VIEW FROM A DISTANCE

To Yvette and Sam

Liz Waller

June 27th 1993

Studies in Austrian Literature, Culture, and Thought

Autobiography Series

VIEW FROM A DISTANCE

By

Lore Lizbeth Waller

ARIADNE PRESS

Library of Congress Cataloging-in-Publication Data

Waller, Lore Lizbeth.
View from a distance / by Lore Lizbeth Waller.
p. cm. -- (Studies in Austrian literature, culture, and thought. Autobiography series)
ISBN 0-929497-61-9
1. Waller, Lore Lizbeth. 2. Jews--Austria--Biography. 3. Refugees, Jewish--Biography. 4. World War, 1939-1945--Personal narratives, Jewish. 5. World War, 1939-1945--Great Britain. 6. Austria--Biography. 7. Great Britain--Biography. I. Title. II. Series.
DS135.A93W188 1993
940.53'159'092--dc20 92-44763
[B] CIP

Cover Design:
Art Director: George McGinnis
Designer, Illustrator: Kristine K. Ahuja

270 Goins Court
Riverside, CA 92507

Printed in the United States of America.
ISBN 0-929497-61-9

This book is dedicated to my grandchildren, Christopher and Lauren, and other young people who have no memory of the most tumultuous time in history.

Acknowledgments

Even though this is my story, I would not have started it, stayed with it or finished it without the help of some very supportive people.

Grateful acknowledgment is made to Vera Lawton, who bought me a tape recorder, insisted I write this book, read it and encouraged me to finish.

Special thanks to Sylvia Rothschild, who taught my autobiography class at Emeritus College, for listening and encouraging me.

Thanks also to my sister-in-law Lola Waller and my friend Jean Rappaport for their suggestions and feedback.

Words cannot expess my appreciation to my daughter Leslie Raftery for her unending dedication to this project and patience with me while I wrote it.

The dedication and valuable editing skills of Sharon Goldinger show on every page; to her, my utmost gratitude and appreciation.

CONTENTS

Preface

PART I

Vienna . . . 3
The Wolfs . . . 9
Eisenstadt . . . 12
The Brauns . . . 17
The Backs . . . 24
Childhood . . . 29
Mother and Father . . . 43
The Divorce . . . 48
Jancsi—My First Love . . . 53
Vacations . . . 57
Prelude to Catastrophe . . . 66
Anschluss and Emigration . . . 72
Czech Interlude
(June 1938 - March 1939) . . . 88

PART II

Arrival in England . . . 99
Culture Shock . . . 103
Not Quite War Yet . . . 106
War . . . 109
1939 - 1940 . . . 111
Wartime London . . . 114
Abergele, North Wales . . . 122
Leamington Spa
(Summer 1941 - Spring 1945) . . . 127
Return to London . . . 134
Victory . . . 137

PART III

Returning to the Continent 141
Germany 144
Esslingen 148
Life in Germany after the War 152
Life Continues 155
Requiem 160
CCD Ends 162
Stars and Stripes 165
My Photo Assignments 169
Reconstruction Begins 180

PART IV

What Happened 185
A Wedding Gift 193
Going Home to a Strange Land 196
Settling in America
(1952 - Present) 199

Preface

Throughout our lives we encounter people and places that have an effect on us. Some more than others. Living through the period of a world war is a devastating and unforgettable experience that no one wants to live through, but everyone needs to hear about.

So many of the personalities and events that challenged our imaginations during that time now seem almost to have been part of a spell—hectic, frenzied, not always good—cast over the entire world.

This is, I hope, no mere chronicling of arresting events, but rather a recreation of a strange time. These were years of high tragedy and comedy, of truth and delusion, of complacency and hysteria.

I wrote this book in the hope that perhaps those who read it will learn and understand a little more about a period of time when life could be so culturally enriched and exciting and then so easily followed by a time when one maniacal man could kill millions.

Life is full of a myriad of experiences, people who touch our lives, times and places to explore, things to do, things to learn, and opportunities to take advantage of. I have tried to do that in my life. And I have tried to share all of those highlights and lowlights with the reader.

Most importantly, while there were indelible marks from the war years, life still went on, and still does. The images of war still persist, but there are new experiences and new memories being created. The war affected. It affected everyone. But we as human beings adjust. We go on. We have to.

Lore Lizbeth Waller
Los Angeles
January 1991

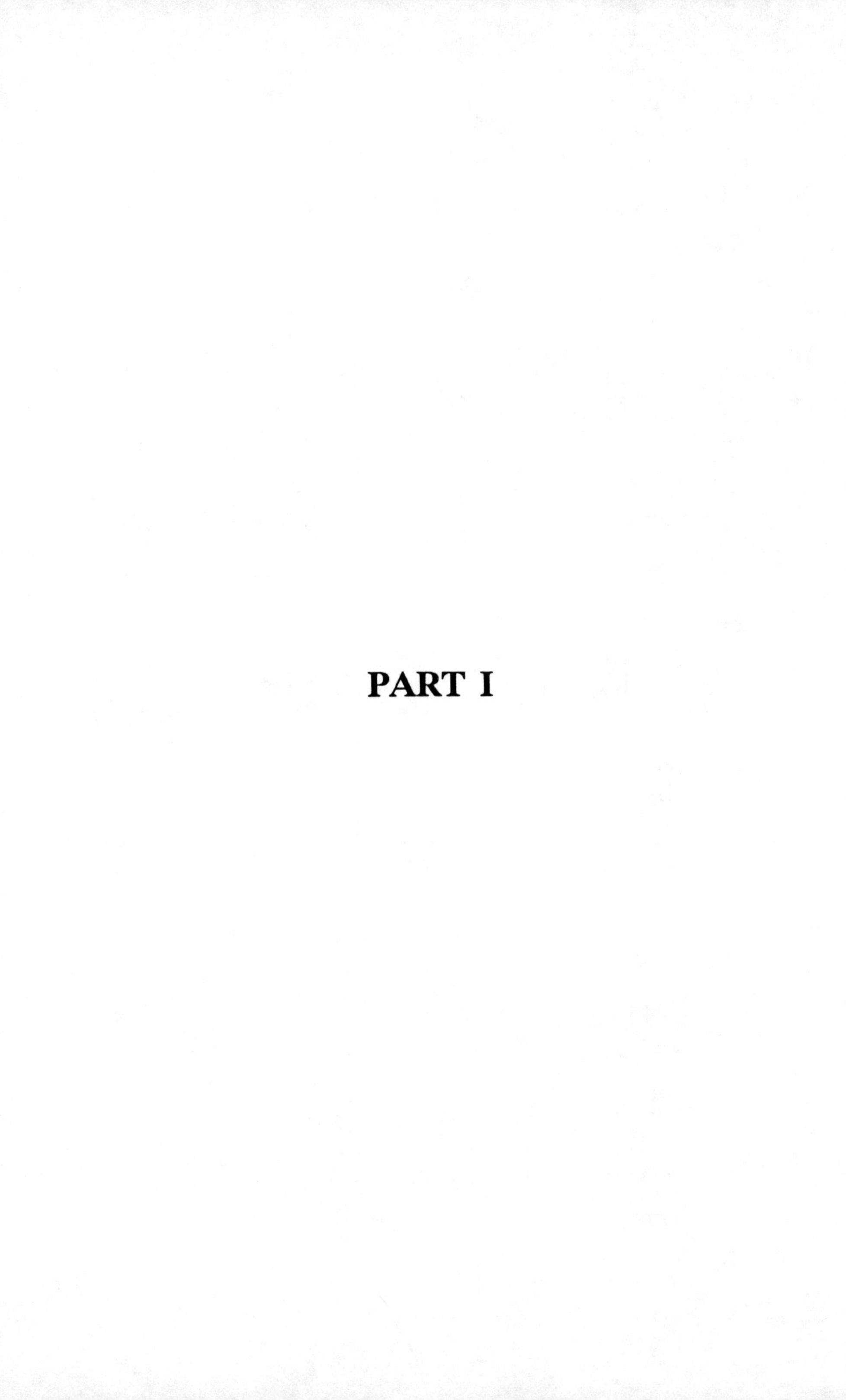

PART I

VIENNA

Nothing is harder for me than to write about Vienna, the beautiful city of my birth that betrayed me. I loved Vienna when I was a child and teenager. I walked through the lovely old streets with the baroque palaces and Biedermeierhouses[1] in awe of the beauty of the city. Now I have bittersweet memories, more bitter than sweet, and yet I feel compelled to write about Vienna. It still is so much a part of me, as no other city could ever be. In many ways I feel I owe so much to Vienna and the atmosphere it created for me and the stimulation it offered.

As American children learn about their heritage—the pilgrims, the revolutionary and civil wars—we learned about our heritage—"the Austrian background." And, even though we loved Austria, the final outcome was that we had to flee for our lives.

As children, we learned about Roman Vienna and that Roman Emperor Marcus Aurelius had his court in Vindobona (Vienna). We were taken to the Roman fortifications at Carnuntum. We learned that Attilla the Hun pillaged the city in 450 A.D., that Charlemagne captured the city in the Ninth Century, and that Babenberg dukes reigned from Vienna. Later, it became the capital of the Holy

---

[1] Biedermeier is an architectural style that was prevalent during the first half of the nineteenth century. It was based on the French Empire style but was simpler and less ornate.

Roman Empire and Habsburg emperors reigned from Vienna for 650 years.

The Hungarians threatened Vienna and the Turks stood twice before the gates of the city. Prince Starhemberg and his army, and later Prince Eugene of Savoy, defeated the Turks. When the Turks finally fled, they left large supplies of coffee; and coffee drinking in coffee houses became a favorite Viennese pastime. Napoleon entered Vienna twice, in 1805 and 1809, and fought two great battles—Aspern and Wagram—at the outskirts of Vienna.[2] In 1814/1815 the Congress of Vienna assembled all the crowned heads of Europe until Napoleon fled Elba and returned to France. He was finally defeated at Waterloo and exiled to the island of St. Helena. All this I learned at school. I also learned about the assassination of the Austrian Archduke Franz Ferdinand at Sarajevo, which precipitated World War I. I loved learning about history at school, but when Hitler marched into Vienna in 1938 somehow he became more history, or rather fate, than all the history I ever studied.

Vienna has not changed much since my youth. When I was a youngster, every Sunday we hiked through the Vienna woods, weather permitting. In winter, we skied through the beautiful woods, usually between Christmas and March. We could ski into the woods from the end of every streetcar line. Now people ride in cars through the woods. You hardly see hikers anymore.

On rainy days, I went through the Kunsthistorische Museum (Museum of Art History). I often went by myself taking in room after room of the marvelous collections of Bruegel, Titian, Rembrandt, Rubens, and Man-

---

[2] The battle of Aspern was won by the Austrians in May 1809. The battle of Wagram was won by Napoleon in July 1809.

tegna. I would go through one room very thoroughly, study every detail of the paintings and then go through the room I had studied the previous week.

I read about the paintings I studied on my Sunday museum visits and had planned to study Art History at the University of Vienna; but I changed my mind after matriculation. The political situation made it clear that I would not have four years to prepare myself for a career. Instead, I attended the Graphical Institute to prepare myself for a career in photography.

My Vienna had a tremendous cultural impact on me, an idealistic teenager. I went to the Opera at least twice a week. Usually I did not sit in my mother's box but stood in the gallery, sometimes with my sister. We heard many operas surrounded by music students and music lovers in the gallery. The talk on the streetcar on the way home from those evenings was about Marie Jeritza or whether Lotte Lehmann had reached the "high C" or not. To this day I still love opera, but there are few opportunities to hear it.

My mother was a fine pianist and my father played the violin. There were weekly chamber music performances at home when we were little. Our guests played the viola and cello.

There was a very special musical tradition in Vienna. Some of the great musical geniuses lived at one time or another in that city: Beethoven, Haydn, Mozart, Schubert, Gluck, Gustav Mahler, Johannes Brahms, Anton Bruckner, Anton von Webern, Johann Strauss (father and son), Arnold Schoenberg, Franz Lehar, and Richard Strauss. They influenced each other and awed me. As a youngster, all this cultural richness was overwhelming, as was the physical beauty of the city.

Vienna is situated at the edge of a plain. The Danube is hardly ever blue, and quite a distance from the city. It is visible only from the Vienna woods. (Now the city has grown to the other bank of the river.) As children, we rarely saw the big, dirty, gray river. Only when we had school excursions to the Napoleonic battlefields, or watched the Graf Zeppelin land, did we cross the river. In later years though, I would paddle downstream in folding boats with groups of young people in the summer. The Vienna woods, west of the city, are lovely. The ground rises imperceptibly and, when going west by train, it rises higher and higher toward the Alps.

The old city had been surrounded by city walls until the middle of the last century when the walls were torn down and the broad boulevard lined with chestnut trees, the Ringstrasse, was built. Along the Ringstrasse are beautiful parks with monuments to the great men of Austrian music and literature. I loved to visit the parks as a teenager. There is a square with lilac bushes so fragrant in spring that you can smell them from a distance. There was a cherry tree in one of the parks. I visited that tree every spring when it was in bloom. It was absolutely magnificent when covered with blossoms.

As a child, I was taken to the house where it was believed that a dragon had roamed. When I was older and allowed to walk by myself, I would go to Drachenhaus (Dragon House) often and look at the lovely old buildings surrounding it. I was enchanted by Vienna's beauty, the culture, the music. All I saw was the romance of it, and rarely the reality of it—the unemployment, the beggars, the antisemitism, the Eichmanns, and the Waldheims (who also grew up in the same city on the Danube at the same time I did).

After the Dollfuss' assassination I became a little more aware that things might not go on as they had. I realized that there was another Vienna (not the idealistic Vienna) and that there was another reality—a harsh, bitter, cold, brutal, cruel reality—which I would confront in March of 1938.

I have been back to Vienna a few times. My half-brother and half-sister live there. But my feelings are very ambivalent when I walk the lovely little streets. Little has changed. The bombed-out buildings were replaced by buildings made from the same stone and of the same height. The bombed roof of St. Stephan's Cathedral has been replaced. The Madonna near the high altar still opens her cloak and little angel heads still peer out of the stone cloak. The parks are well tended. The opera house has been rebuilt. The Lippizzan stallions of the Spanish riding school still prance every Sunday. But the Jews are gone and the role of the Viennese in this was not a noble one. They were cruel, sadistic, vicious, and uncaring.

A few years ago, one of my mother's cousins took me to a coffee house. The food and the pastries were as delicious as ever. At the table next to ours, I noticed an elderly blond woman with a little dog. I smiled at her and the little dog. She looked at me. Her gaze was so cold, so full of hate. I knew what she thought. I felt paralyzed that so much hate still existed.

I am very torn between the rose-colored memories and the bitter reality. I owe Vienna, or rather my Viennese parents, the cultural background in which I was raised. Yet I had to leave when I was young without the university education I had hoped for, but enough cultural upbringing to sustain me in the strange life I led—really, the four lives I have lived:

> The pampered, romantic child of Vienna from a broken home; sickness; the Nazis.

The confused refugee during the war and bombardment in England. Years of poverty, uncertainties, anxieties, hardships and, of course, also fun.

The news photographer in postwar Germany and all the adventures that came with that profession.

The American housewife and working mother.

Vienna was the foundation and beginning of all that.

THE WOLFS

My parents were divorced in 1936, and since my parents separation in 1930, my sister and I lived with our mother. We had hardly any contact with father's family after I was eleven and then it was unpleasant.

I particularly loved my mother's family. My great-grandmother, Hermine Wolf, was the most beloved and admired member of mother's clan. I was too young when she died to really understand why she was so precious to us. She just was. Her huge family adored her.

She was born in 1845 and died in 1932. She had given birth to eleven children. Nine lived to be adults—two sons and seven daughters. One great aunt drowned in a tragic coach accident in Lake St. Moritz, Switzerland. My mother's mother died rather young and I have only vague memories of her. My mother's aunts lived very close to their mother. One great aunt and great-grandmother's bachelor son, Uncle Sandor, lived with their mother.

The family had two homes, one in Vienna and another in Eisenstadt, an Austrian provincial capital. The Princes Esterhazy had big estates there and Josef Haydn had been their court composer. The Wolfs were their wine suppliers. The Wolf family owned property in Eisenstadt since the reign of Josef II (1780-1790) when Jews were first permitted to own land in the Habsburg realms.

My great-grandmother (Urgrossmama) was raised by her grandparents. Her parents had died in an epidemic. When she married my great-grandfather, Ignatz Wolf, a wine merchant, she received as a dowry an addition built to the old family house. The house was quite large by then. The old wing was built in the 16-17th century. The new addition was Victorian. The vineyards, fields, gardens, tennis court and playground were quite a distance from the house. But that did not matter to three generations of children who were taken by coach to play there under the supervision of nannies and relatives. My grandmother (and her siblings), her children and her children's children all enjoyed playing there.

My great-grandmother had twenty-five grandchildren. Most of my mother's cousins were university trained men and women, though my mother was not. Not too many of these highly educated women married. All the men served in the Austrian army during World War I. Two were killed, among them my mother's brother Ernst.

The Wolfs were a happy family. The old great-aunts were fat, little, witty women who loved to tell jokes about themselves and others. They crocheted and embroidered and were busy with the vast household in Eisenstadt where the family gathered every summer. Some came for a few days, others for a few weeks. There was a constant coming and going of relatives. More houses were gradually acquired by family members since the original purchase in 1790. These houses were adjacent to the original Wolf house. Uncle Sandor added another wing to accommodate his vast collection of antiques.

Those times were wonderful. Life in Eisenstadt seemed to us like an unending summer presided over by Urgrossmama. When I knew her, she was a stout little woman, although according to photographs, she was quite pretty in her youth. She always wore long black dresses and a hat tied under her chin. She went for daily walks attended to by stout, little women (either her housekeeper or one of her daughters) also in black dresses. As children in Vienna, we were usually taken to a park to play and Urgrossmama often came to watch us.

Urgrossmama and I talked often, although I cannot remember any particular conversation with her. She seemed quiet and passive. During the school year when we were in Vienna, I loved to visit her in the afternoons. I would arrive unannounced and was ushered into a flower-filled room where she soon appeared. She always sat in the same chair. I kissed her hand. She never kissed or hugged me, or came to our home. I always went to her. She never demonstrated her feelings, but her mere presence, her great age, her reputation in the family created such feelings of awe and love in me. I still have two lockets she gave me as a child. Five of her grandchildren (mother's cousins) are still alive.

After she died, I became very close with my great-aunts. I loved to visit them, and felt loved and supported by them during the difficult years of my parents' divorce.

Though my parents' divorce caused me much pain, I felt loved and sheltered by my mother's vast family. It was not long before I lost them all. Our whole life, the world we knew, our whole existence would collapse. We would soon have to flee for our lives. We would have to leave behind the world we knew, and seek new lands, new lives, and new friends as well as learn new languages.

EISENSTADT

Eisenstadt is the capital of the Austrian State of Burgenland (Castleland). It is surrounded by soft rolling hills. It has been, and still is, a rather dull little town. In my youth, Eisenstadt had a population of ten thousand people. It is situated close to the Hungarian border and belonged to Hungary before World War I. The population then consisted mostly of Hungarians. The plebiscite of 1921 awarded it to Austria. Most of the population was bilingual—Hungarian and German. My old great-aunts spoke German with a strong Hungarian accent.

In the center of the town is the enormous yellow castle of the Princes Esterhazy with beautiful grounds surrounding it. The gardens are open to the public today and even have a public swimming pool. In my childhood, they were off limits to the citizens of Eisenstadt. The grounds are lovely with manicured lawns, a lily pond, greenhouses, colorful flower beds, and quiet secluded walks. Not far from the castle is the charming old baroque house where Eisenstadt's most honored citizen, Josef Haydn, lived when he was the court musician to the Esterhazys. There are flowers in the flower boxes outside every window. The Haydn house is a museum now. On the outskirts of Eisenstadt is a round church famous for its architecture. Josef Haydn is buried there.

Judengasse (Jewish Street) does not exist today. All the Jews have disappeared. In the 1920s and 1930s my Granduncle Sandor, as president of the Jewish community, was instrumental in closing off the street to traffic between Friday night and Saturday night to preserve the peace of the holy day (the Sabbath). A chain at one end of the little street and a gate at the other prevented traffic from moving through Judengasse. The same chain and gate were used during the Middle Ages to confine the Jewish population within the medieval ghetto. The houses owned by my family stood just outside the former ghetto.

When I was a child, radios, telephones and newspapers were available, but Eisenstadt still had a town crier who made his rounds every evening. Our parents could not get us to go to bed until he had completed his rounds. I do not remember what he cried about, whether it was local gossip or world news, but it hardly made a difference to me. He had a deep booming voice and I was very impressed.

Eisenstadt, of course, had a fire department. I remember the fire drills vividly—there was great excitement, whistling, hooting, clattering and out came the fire engines, not motorized, but propelled by manpower. They had no hoses, just buckets. Fortunately, no fire threatened the town. Eisenstadt also had a town idiot. There was great agitation among us children when the poor fellow made his way through the streets.

Part of the house owned by the Wolf family had been built in the sixteenth or seventeenth century, but the interior had been modernized and brought up-to-date. There were telephones and electricity, running water and bathrooms, but no drinking water. For cooking and washing dishes, the water had to be boiled; drinking water had to be fetched from the well and carried in two barrels hanging from a long pole on strong shoulders. Bath water was drawn from the tap. As a youngster, I did not think much about it, but now I wonder how hygienic bathing was in Eisenstadt. Apparently, no harm was ever done.

Our quarters in the family house adjoined the museum where my mother's uncle had his collection of antiques. On rainy days we were not allowed to go to the rather distant play area on the property, but played on top of a tower next to the museum. To get to the tower, however, we had to walk through the museum and go through a trap door that led to the Narrenturm (fool's tower). I always ran through the collection because I was too scared to walk. The reason for my fear was the head of an Egyptian mummy; it had no nose but was otherwise well preserved with very distinct features. My uncle had excavated in Egypt and Pompeii and amassed all kinds of treasures, amongst them the fear-inspiring head.

One day, there was a great fuss and we were punished for touching and shifting things in the museum. I knew I had not done it. I was too scared to linger on my way to the tower. I suspect that other children, too, tried to get through that place as quickly as they could. Maybe the cleaning people moved things. In any case, we were scolded and punished and the old great-aunts were very upset with us. So was the curator.

In the part of the house that served as our vacation quarters was an old piece of furniture. It was triangular shaped to fit into a corner. My sister tried to get into one of the top shelves while standing on one of the bottom shelves. She did not realize that it was not one, but two pieces fitted on top of each other. The top part came crashing down on her. It had been filled with jars of pickled cucumbers. They all broke. My sister, fortunately, was not hurt but the old aunts were furious—all that wasted effort of pickling and preserving (which was a great summer activity in Eisenstadt). The penetrating smell of that mishap remained with us for the rest of our vacation.

Another incident happened when I was sick one day (and not allowed to join the other children who were driven off by a horse-drawn carriage to the family play area). However, they soon came back to the house with the old aunts. The children had been found eating poisonous berries. The old aunts tried to induce vomiting by sticking their fingers into the children's mouths, but to no avail. All the children were taken to the local doctor to have their stomachs pumped, and I was left at the house gloating.

My great-grandmother was religious, but my parents were not. My sister and I grew up without religion until it was suggested that we attend the little synagogue in Judengasse. Men and women were separated. We were upstairs and it gave us a great vantage point of the activities downstairs and to ogle the cute boys there. We started attending regularly during summer vacations. It was probably our puberty rather than religious devotion that created the interest.

In our early teens, the vineyards and grounds the family owned became a vast playground to play "hide and seek" and "cops and robbers." We played endlessly and had lots of fabulous places to hide.

One day we were looking for our friend, Erich Geschwindt, for hours only to discover him up in a tree. He refused to come down. His brother had to climb up and we heard them whispering. Erich stayed up but his brother came down and ran off to town. Erich had dispatched him to get a bottle of blue ink. The ink was taken up into the tree. Erich had torn his blue pants and the ink was used to paint his derriere to match them. Only after the end of this operation did Erich come down from his perch.

Erich was a nice boy and very intelligent. During that summer he was a little attracted to me. We may have been thirteen or fourteen years old. My friend Liesl, however, was in love with him and to this day she remembers her frustrated love for Erich. Poor Erich did not survive the Nazis, nor did his brother.

Those summers in Eisenstadt were idyllic and unforgettable. We led a charmed life. The doom that followed could not be anticipated.

The large castle and the memorials to Haydn are still there. The Jewish population is gone—wiped out by the Nazis. Only one Jewish man returned after the war. In order to be able to say his prayers, he was given a dispensation from the chief Rabbi of Austria to pray without the other nine men necessary to form a minyan. He is dead now. I heard that another Jewish family recently moved to Eisenstadt.

THE BRAUNS

My grandfather, Josef Braun (1855-1929), was an awe-inspiring man. He was very formal, very elegant. (It was beneath his dignity to carry a package. Everything had to be sent from the store to him.) He had been widowed twice. My grandmother, one of the many Wolf sisters, died young and he married again (soon after her death), a much younger woman. Ilse was beautiful. My mother was heartbroken that Grandfather forgot her mother so soon. Ilse became very ill shortly after their wedding and my good mother helped nurse her. Ilse died miserably of brain cancer. She became blind, then deaf, and suffered terribly. At the time my grandfather died, there was yet another younger ladyfriend to whom he left quite a bit of money and Persian carpets.

My grandfather inherited a brewery from his father who had been an engineer and built and owned the first railroad in what is now Czechoslovakia. The railroad venture had been very costly and a financial failure for my great-grandfather. From the money he salvaged he bought a small brewery, in Jarosov, that had been part of a monastery.[3] My grandfather enlarged, modernized and transformed it into a well-run profitable business. There was a malt factory attached to it.

This line of the Braun family prospered. My grandfather spent most of his time near the brewery. My

---

[3] Jarosov is a small Czech village in Moravia near Uherske Hradiste.

mother and her three brothers were born in a little town three miles away. My grandfather maintained a house in the little town of Uherske Hradiste and, later, also an apartment in Vienna so my mother could attend the ball season there.

After my parents married they moved into an apartment next to my grandfather's. A door connected the two apartments. On Sundays, when my grandfather was in Vienna, my sister and I were dressed in blue or pink silk dresses and taken to see him. We kissed his hand. He got up from his chair ceremoniously, took a key from the gold chain that decorated his waistcoat, unlocked a chest of drawers and took out a piece of paper. He rolled it into a cone, then repeated the ritual and filled both cones with candy. He patted us on our heads and soon we were dismissed. There was a less severe side to him, though. He built us a wonderful, beautifully detailed doll house.

As a young man, grandfather was an excellent swimmer. He rescued two men, whose boat had capsized in the fast flowing river, from certain death. He got an award for bravery. Later he received a title "Kaiserlicher Rat" (Imperial Counsel). (He may have bought the title.) When I was a child, Austria was a republic. People called him either Rat Braun (Councilman) or, those more familiar with him, Josi. During the Austrian monarchy he had been a beer supplier to the court.

He traveled widely, frequently taking my mother with him before she married. He had taken her to Egypt and to various spas hoping that she would meet eligible young men. However, he did not give mother his permission to marry the young man of her choice, Schonsky, who was the son of an employee and not Jewish.

Much later, mother married another man of her choice, Dr. Emmerich Back (my father), an extremely good looking, charming, fortune hunter. Her parents and both sides of the family advised against this union and my Mother regretted it later.

My grandfather employed two of his brothers in the brewery. The third was his partner, and the fourth brother was a lawyer in Vienna. He died of tuberculosis, that dreaded disease that also killed one of grandfather's sisters. She was quite young at the time of her death. Grandfather had two more sisters. Aunt Emma was a sweet old maid. She made wonderful little flower arrangements out of bread dough and painted these small flower baskets in many colors. She never failed to bring one of them when she visited us, when we were little children. Then there was Aunt Esti, sweet, kind and melancholic. Two of her daughters were in an insane asylum. Aunt Emma, Uncle Heinrich, Aunt Esti and most of her descendants were later killed in Theresienstadt. The great-aunts and Uncle Heinrich (who always pinched our maids' behinds) were very old at the time of their deportation to Theresienstadt. Poor things!

In contrast to the witty, bubbly, stout Wolf great-aunts and uncles, the Brauns were serious, almost severe, tall and thin. My grandfather's brother Ludwig, one of the two brothers employed by grandfather, had a love affair with Mother's French governess, Madi. Ludwig wanted to marry her but my grandfather would not permit this union at first. Ludwig and Madi had two sons; only after the second son was born did Ludwig marry her. And although grandfather threatened Ludwig with dismissal, he was able to keep his job after marrying Madi. Madi was shunned and treated as an outcast by all the Brauns with the exception of my mother. Madi died quite young. Her two sons were small children at the time and spent much of their childhood and adolescent years with us.

At the time of the Anschluss,[4] the boys heard about the shabby treatment of their mother and did not want to have anything further to do with the Brauns. They were only half Jewish and looked like typical Nazis, but they suffered badly during Nazi times. The older brother was sent to a camp, but survived. Whenever I have visited Vienna he has seen me, but no one else of the surviving Brauns. My cousins are still angry because my grandfather interfered with so many lives with disastrous consequences.

Grandfather Braun was a very wealthy man, yet his sisters lived very frugally in Vienna. They still had gaslight in their flats. But in the little town near the brewery (close to Uherske Hradiste) they lived in a lovely Biedermeier house, their parents' home. Field Marshal Radetzky (immortalized by Johann Strauss in his "Radetzky March,") took up quarters in that house during the Austro-Prussian War of 1866.

In this little town stands a very large castle owned by the grand dukes of Lichtenstein. A duke fell in love with one of grandfather's cousins and married her. She became the grand duchess of Lichtenstein, but the present reigning duke is not her descendant as she died without issue.

One of grandfather's cousins was Victor Adler. He founded the Austrian social democratic party. His bust is still standing in front of the Austrian Parliament building in Vienna. Victor's son, Friedrich Adler, committed a political assassination. In 1916, he killed the prime minister in a restaurant. He was condemned to death, but the sentence was later commuted leaving him free to be involved in red politics.

---

[4] The Anschluss was the annexation of Austria by the Germans in 1938.

Socialist writers, Heinrich Braun and his wife Lilly, were grandfather's cousins. (Lilly Braun descended from Napoleon's brother, Jerome, the King of Westphalia.) Their son, an extremely talented writer, Otto Braun, was killed in World War I. Mother's brother, Ernst, was also killed in World War I. Two of my cousins, born after his death, were named for him.

Grandfather was not at all proud of this socialist connection—he was a capitalist through and through. He was, however, proud of his cousin, Henrietta Szold, who was an American. Her parents had immigrated to the United States in 1856. Henrietta's mother was the sister of grandfather's mother. Henrietta became the foremost Jewish woman of her time. She was the founder of the Hadassah and the Youth Aliah. She personally saved the lives of thousands of Jewish children from annihilation by the Nazis. I met her once when she was very old and visited Vienna. I am still in touch with her Baltimore relatives.

My mother had three brothers, Fritz, Kurt and Ernst. They all served in the Austrian army during World War I. Fritz was taken prisoner by the Russians and was presumed dead. The Russians did not release him from the Siberian prisoner of war camp. However, in 1921, he fled via China and India. He arrived in Vienna a week after his mother had died believing that he had been killed during the war. His cousin, Louise, a Wolf descendant, had been friendly with him before the war. She waited for him all those years convinced that he was alive. After his return, my grandfather insisted that Fritz marry Louise. This marriage proved a disaster. Louise was very intellectual and very sweet but slightly crazy. She had a Ph.D. in botany. Fritz and Louise were first cousins. Being so closely related, their union produced a daughter, Susi, who was sick all her life. Susi needed several surgeries and was even taken to the United States for medical treatment and a colostomy.

Fritz was the most devoted and kind father to his daughter. He tutored her at home since Susi was unable to attend school. Fritz was a chemist and the brewer in the family enterprise. He was also a diabetic.

After the Nazis came to power in Czechoslovakia the family fled to Israel. They left with no money and had to live in one room in Haifa. Uncle Fritz suffered from these cramped living arrangements. His wife and sick daughter made him very nervous and he was unhappy. After the war, Fritz found a good job as a biologist in Teheran. But he came down with a bacterial infection, after which his diabetes became uncontrollable, and he died miserably. I loved my Uncle Fritz—he was a wonderful man, sweet, witty and kind. He had great intellect and very little luck.

Louise returned to Vienna about 1960 and worked for years at the University as a botanist. Her special field of expertise included mosses and ferns. She died recently at a very great age. Although Susi was married for a short time, she had a sad, short life. She died of an insulin overdose in her early forties.

Uncle Ernst, Mother's favorite brother, was extremely handsome and very tall. He had been sick with tuberculosis as a youngster and spent several years in a sanatorium in Davos, Switzerland. He was cured and discharged from the sanatorium in 1914, volunteered for the army and was killed the following year. He was riding through a Russian village when he was shot off his horse by snipers. He was only twenty-three years old. Mother often showed me the medal that was awarded to him posthumously.

Before going to war he had given Mother his dog, Nicki. Nicki was our childhood playmate until he was run over by a car.

Uncle Kurt, mother's youngest brother, became the director of the brewery after my grandfather died in 1929. He fled to Israel with his wife and son after the Nazi takeover of Czechoslovakia. I helped their daughter Herta emigrate to England. She spent the war years in England and now lives in Wales. After the war, she helped her parents and brother join her there.

Finally, the family was reunited after years and years of separation. Uncle Kurt and his wife Gretl are dead now. Herta's brother, Ernst, is a scientist and moved back to Vienna a few years ago. The Kurt Brauns operated a laundry in Israel, and times were anything but easy for them there.

All generations of the Brauns had long narrow faces, aquiline noses and rather aristocratic looking features. I own a painting of an ancestor, done around 1830, that shows the family characteristics. When members of the old generation were still alive they would divulge the secret of the aristocratic appearance—it was to be found in our illegitimate descent from English royalty. King Richard, the Lion-Hearted, held prisoner in Austria after the third crusade, got a nice Jewish girl into trouble. Their descendants were named Loewenrosen (Lion-rose).

The lion and the rose are on the England's royal shield. Who knows? In any case, there is the name and the appearance!

THE BACKS

My grandfather, Leopold Back, died long before I was born. I do not know when he died. My grandmother's maiden name was Hermine Feuer. They both came from Hungary.

Grandfather Back had been a professor at the Academy of Music in Vienna and concert master under Johann Strauss. My grandmother, Hermine Back, was a small, regal-looking woman, with silvery hair piled high on her small head. She always wore elegant, old fashioned clothes and white, lacy fichus.[5] She was quite young when she was widowed. All her children had professional training except the oldest, Else. Her daughter, Yella, was an accountant in a large prestigious firm and lived with her mother.

One of my father's brothers, Oscar, had been a child prodigy—a famous violinist. He had given concerts all over Europe. As he became older he did not like the concert stage anymore. He was a shy man and suffered from stage fright. Teaching became his life. He taught master music classes in Amsterdam and the Hague. Students flocked to him from all over the world. Among his friends were violinists Igor and David Oistrach, as well as Yehudi Menuhin.

---

[5] A fichu was a neckerchief or a small shawl made of sheer white material or lace that was worn to cover a low neckline.

Music was his world and his friends were musicians. He was sought out to judge music competitions. In his old age, he received many honors. A great celebration was held at the famous concert hall, Concertgebouw, in Amsterdam on the occasion of his eightieth birthday. Queen Juliana of the Netherlands bestowed honors and a knighthood on him. The former Queen of Belgium, Elisabeth (widow of King Albert I), was an ardent music lover and a great friend of my uncle's. She visited his home many times. He had a charming small house in Amsterdam. He married and divorced a Dutch woman. His children were raised in Brussels.

He was a lovely man, very impressive looking with a long mane of hair. Everybody who knew him simply adored him. Every year at Christmas he would send me a box of chocolates. The last one arrived long after he was gone. I remember from my childhood when he and my older cousins visited us in Vienna. Oh, the excitement and joy of having our older cousins stay with us!

During World War II he was in hiding in Holland; not even his children knew where he was. Uncle Oscar suffered from arteriosclerosis necessitating the amputation of a leg. Mercifully, he died when the second leg was amputated in 1963.

After Uncle Oscar's death a fund was created in his name to help poor young music students. Every two years a concert is given at the Concertgebouw to raise money for the Oscar Back Foundation.

One of my father's sisters, Hilda, was a promising concert pianist. She died very young of a broken heart after her husband, also a pianist, was killed in World War I. Two of my father's brothers had law degrees from the University of Vienna.

Father, too, had a doctorate in law but never practiced his legal profession. My father and all his brothers were eventually divorced—at a time when divorce was very rare. My grandmother had eight daughters-in-law from four sons! The brothers were not conventional husbands, but they were marvelous sons, considerate and loving to their mother. My grandmother was venerated and honored by her children and probably supported by them.

Grossmama (grandmother) Back was very nice to us when we were small children. She took us for outings to the Prater, the large amusement park in Vienna. We visited her often in her beautiful apartment in Wassergasse with the Boesendorfer piano that had belonged to Aunt Hilda. But once my parents' divorce proceedings started mother did not permit us to see her again.

Here I must tell of my shameful behavior toward Grossmama Back. I saw her once on the street of Vienna—she did not live too far from us. She was quite old by then and I, her granddaughter, pretended not to see her. We children had been drawn so deeply into this divorce that we became biased. All we could see was how profoundly our mother suffered. Now that I am a grandmother myself, I can understand how deeply I hurt the old woman.

Uncle Richard, the father of my cousin Hilde, lived in Berlin.[6] In the early twenties there was a big Back family gathering in Garmisch-Partenkirchen. The inflation in Germany was at its height but had not hit Austria yet. It was very cheap to stay in luxurious hotels with nannies and all the relatives. Uncle Richard showed up with his beautiful mistress, Mirette, whom he later married. Mirette proved to be the proverbial bad stepmother to

---

[6] My cousin Hilde was named after my Aunt Hilda who died at a very young age.

Hilde. Richard, Mirette and Hilde fled to New York after the Nazis came to power in Germany. Uncle Richard, and later Hilde, died there. Mirette returned to Belgium with her new husband, twenty years younger than herself. Hilde's daughters are married to doctors in Florida and I hear from them occasionally.

Uncle Alfred had one daughter, Hansi. She went to London when the Nazis came to Vienna and was never heard of again. She had a difficult youth. Her parents, too, were getting divorced. Her mother not able to face this, committed suicide. She killed herself in a suicide pact with a young man in a hotel room on the eve of her divorce trial. The Vienna papers reported every sordid detail.

Uncle Alfred, I believe, was not very successful as a lawyer. I do not know where he was during World War II. However, after the War, he was in Vienna and married again. He, too, had to have a leg amputated due to arteriosclerosis.

We were not allowed to see Aunt Yella after my parents separated but I became very friendly with her after the war. She had married a Dutchman to get out of Austria. She was in hiding during the Nazi occupation of Holland, but somehow survived. I believe she had false papers. That may have aided in her ability to survive. She was a lovely intelligent woman. She died around 1960.

The oldest of my grandmother Back's children was my father's sister, Else. She was married to Oscar Fasal, a very nice gentleman, who had a hard time making a living. Else worked as a dressmaker in their apartment. They had two children, my cousins Hans and Gretl. Gretl was a beautiful girl, a little older than me. We did not see them after my parents' divorce proceedings began. Sometimes we would bump into them in Vienna, but did not associate with them anymore. Gretl, her husband and parents were sent to Theresienstadt. Poor Gretl and her husband did not survive the Nazis. Else and her husband returned to Vienna where Oscar Fasal died soon after liberation. Else remained a broken woman. She kept house for my father for a while. When I visited my father in Vienna in 1947, Else prepared marvelous dishes for me.

During the war, my father was in hiding in Hungary. He had false papers and a Catholic wife.

CHILDHOOD

My first conscious memories are of my lying in my little crib and looking out of the window where white little stars came floating down through a gray sky and settled on the window sill.

I was born in Vienna in 1918. My mother had a very difficult forceps delivery. I was a great disappointment to my parents, especially to my father, who wanted a boy to carry on the family name and its musical tradition. When I was five years old he tried to convert tone-deaf me into a child prodigy—alas, totally without success. My parents did not like my looks because the difficult delivery left its marks on my initial appearance. I grew up an extremely shy, sensitive, little girl. The initial deformities disappeared but my little soul was bitterly sore. I heard so much from my parents of their disappointment in me.

When I was very small my parents rented a summer house not far from Vienna. I must have been two years old, with blond curls and big black eyes. In all the photographs, I wore white shoes, which were always cleaned with a special white "stuff." I remember one time, I had gotten hold of this shoe cleaner and played with it in the garden where lovely, tempting, rain puddles had accumulated. I was warned not to throw it into the puddle or I would be punished. The temptation was too great and I threw it into the muddy water. I was hauled into the house. My father appeared with his walking stick. Seeing what was about to happen I ran off. He pursued me and we ran 'round and 'round the dining room table. He caught up with me, of course. I ended up on his knees with my pants down and I received a sound thrashing. For what offense?

My sister Hedy was delivered at home and my first introduction to her is vivid in my memory. There was "that" little baby lying in my Mother's arms. I felt sad and replaced and walked over to her, not to kiss her as I was told but, to pull her hair. My parents were disgusted with me.

As a child, I hated milk and all milk products. My grandmother Back was very concerned about my well-being and when we spent summer vacations with her, I was made to drink milk and buttermilk. My protestations were fierce. I screamed and kicked, threw myself on the ground and made terrific scenes to Grandmama's great embarrassment. As soon as I had a say in the matter, I gave up milk products altogether. (Now that I have severe osteoporosis, I wish I had listened to her.)

I began my piano lessons when I was five years old. I could not read yet, but Father had great musical expectations for me. We had a Bluenthner grand piano at home. My Father would sit with me while I practiced and became very dissatisfied and irritated when I did not do well, which was almost always. It was pure torture, and more so when my piano teacher, Fräulein von Fleischmann, became the laughingstock of the neighborhood maids, as they watched her biweekly approach to my house out of their open windows. This was in the early twenties when the fashion was short skirts and bobbed hair. Fräulein von Fleischmann clung to the fashions of the 1890s. She wore long skirts, a lace-necked, long-sleeved blouse, a long chain on her chest and her hair piled up high. I was mortified to be associated with the laughingstock of the neighborhood. My piano career ended abruptly when I was only seven years old.

In my early years, my parents led a very active social life and entertained a lot. We had musical evenings at home. My parents also went out to balls. One evening, my mother came into the nursery in a beautiful fancy ball gown, in a style a la Marie Antoinette, complete with white wig and a beauty spot. She seemed like a fairy queen to me. Later, I was told that my parents had learned that evening that my father's bookkeeper had absconded with the assets of my father's bank. He lost a fortune.

Much of the time my sister and I were left in the care of nannies or governesses. I am sad for my mother now, because she did not have much time for us. But when we were sick (and I was sick a lot), she read to me, cooked special food, or wrapped me in hot or cold wet sheets, whatever was required for whatever ailed me (at a time when there were no antibiotics). Being sick was a time for special attention and not altogether unwelcome. I was pampered and watched over.

Through the first grade I was tutored at home with my cousins Julia Schur and Heidi Goldschmidt, and another girl, Mariechen Gerngross, who was later killed by the Nazis. After that I went to private school for two years. That caused terrible anxieties. I worried myself sick over homework assignments and whether I had all the things together that I needed for school the next day.

About that time, I had a frightening dream. I dreamed that the devil himself came down from the sky in a whirl of dust and noise and exploded. I screamed and woke up to find I had wet my bed. Years later, I often thought of that frightening dream when the bombs came raining down on us during the bombardments of London during the war.

One day, I had to clean the blackboard at school with a little boy. He was washing it and I was to lower it and put a plug in so it would not slip down. Somehow I missed and the blackboard fell down and shattered. A note was sent home. I had to stand in the corner and my parents had to pay for a new blackboard. I felt so humiliated and upset. I was sure that I was the worst and most unhappy child in the world. How could they make so much fuss over something that was clearly unintentional?

I was terribly shy for many years and lacked self-confidence. Once, when I was invited to a children's party by the same little boy I shared the blackboard disaster with, I hid the whole time in a stairwell rather than enjoy the party.

We had very few playmates in Vienna. Sometimes we were taken to homes of my mother's friends who had children our age. I still remember the puppet performances, on little theater stages, they gave for Hedy and me. Because of the lonely winters in Vienna, our summer visits to Eisenstadt became very important.

We had a Fräulein (governess) for several years. She played with us, took us to the park and shared our room. Her favorite topic of conversation focused on her fiancee. When the day of her wedding finally arrived, mother attended and brought her a gift. The bride and groom went off on their honeymoon to an Austrian resort. Several weeks later she visited mother and invited her to her wedding! Mother was perplexed. She learned from Fräulein that on the way to the resort, Fräulein became very ill. She needed an immediate appendectomy and fell in love with her doctor. Her first marriage had not been consummated and was annulled. Mother attended the second wedding, too.

Besides nannies, maids and other help, my mother hired a pretty young cook. Lily was a peasant girl and came to us when we were quite little. She was very nice to us then. My mother, a famous hostess in Vienna and well-trained in domestic skills by her mother, trained Lily. She became a very good cook, but later my mother's nemesis.

When I was about nine years old, I developed symptoms of a pre-tubercular condition. After years of delicate health and all the childhood diseases, it was decided that I should be treated in Switzerland. There had been so many cases of tuberculosis in the Braun family that my parents were very worried and arrangements were made for mother and me to spend three months in Arosa. This was a very happy time for me because I had my mother to myself.

The trip to Arosa, Switzerland was full of fun. My mother's young cousins, just a little older than I, and their father, Uncle Ludwig, traveled with us from Vienna to Chur. I was impressed by the endlessly long tunnels through the Alps. It was a very long train trip indeed and it was interrupted in Innsbruck where we did a little sightseeing and spent the night. It was a rather noisy night—laughter, squeaking, and running bath water was heard next door. My mother told Uncle Ludwig about it at breakfast. Of course, at nine years old, I did not understand, but reflecting upon it now, it seems that a pair of noisy lovers were at it all night long.

In Arosa, mother wanted us to stay in a luxury hotel, so we went to the Grand Hotel. It turned out to be a sanatorium for people with tuberculosis, and once we got there, it was hard to get out and transfer to a regular hotel. My treatment included lying on a terrace exposed only to indirect sunlight. I talked to people on the balconies next to mine but I could not see them because of the partitions. Some of the people had been in the sanatorium for many years. There was no cure for tuberculosis then. My neighbor had been there for twenty years. Terrible operations were performed.[7] There were two young girls on the same floor as I. One day the girls piled up their love letters on the floor of their room, set them ablaze and the room caught fire. There was great excitement at the sanatorium.

After we parted in Chur, mother's young cousins and Uncle Ludwig spent their vacation in Flims, Switzerland. A very lively correspondence, with drawings and decals, developed amongst us. This was a delightful way for me to occupy the lonely time on my balcony.

Eventually my mother and I were allowed to leave the sanatorium and we moved to the Hotel Valsana. I still had to lie on a shaded balcony and was only allowed to walk one hour a day. I read Dr. Doolittle.

Arosa was, and still is, a beautiful Alpine resort. There are several lakes in the little town. I remember seeing my first fireworks there. They were lovely. My mother and I sat at the edge of a lake watching them. That same evening my mother entertained me with a story of a corpse that had been fished out of the lake the previous week, describing in detail how swollen it was, etc. I had terrible nightmares after that.

I heard my first English spoken there. Miss Maser was the English speaker. I was very impressed listening to her not knowing that English would be the language of my future.

One day, the papers were filled with stories about Vienna; there was unrest. The Palace of Justice had been

---

[7] For example, the pneumothorax procedure was used as a treatment for tuberculosis. I believe this procedure involved collapsing a lung in order to heal it.

set afire and many people had been killed. My mother was very worried that something happened to my father. She assumed correctly that he was in the thick of things and we did not know on whose side he was; but he was unharmed.

In the Hotel Valsana, I was permitted to take meals with the rest of the hotel guests and they could visit me on my shaded balcony. A famous Austrian actor, Albert Bassermann, was a guest at the hotel and I felt elated being in the same building with him.

One day, I woke up with high fever and pain in my side. A local doctor was consulted. I had an inflamed appendix and immediate surgery was advised. My mother did not trust the Swiss doctors. In a panic, she packed and arranged to take me back to Vienna. I was not allowed to walk and had to be in a wheelchair for train connections. This made a lasting impression on me. A telegram had been sent to my father, asking him to fetch us from the West station in Vienna.

On the way back to Vienna we changed trains in Chur. With the use of the wheelchair, we traveled through without interruption. We arrived in Vienna early on a Sunday morning in 1927, but Father was not at the station. We took a taxi, arrived at our home, and rang the doorbell. No answer. We rang again. It must have been noon by then. Finally, Father, in a nightgown, appeared at the door, astonished, perplexed, and perhaps embarrassed. The telegram had not been delivered. Suddenly, Lily (our young and very pretty cook) also in night clothes, came to the door from the direction of my parents' bedroom. My mother did not seem to notice. Only during my parents' divorce was this scene mentioned again.

A specialist was consulted and it was not necessary to remove my appendix. My schooling was resumed. I had missed quite a bit of time from the traditional school year by being in Switzerland so long.

I remember my school teacher very fondly. Fräulein Mott told us that now that Austria was a republic, and not an empire, there would be no more wars. She did not know that one did not need a Kaiser to start a war. Little did she know that Hitler could do it too, causing even more suffering and destruction. In the spring of 1928, Fräulein Mott got married and there was a beautiful celebration which we children prepared for weeks.

After my grandfather's death, we lived in the apartment he had occupied. Before, we lived in the adjoining apartment. The two apartments were connected by a door. Grandfather used his apartment in Vienna only occasionally. He spent most of the year in Czechoslovakia near his brewery. A maid lived in the apartment and took care of it; but when grandfather was out of town the connecting door was locked.

There were some funny moments throughout my childhood. A few stand out more than others.

One summer, mother, Hedy and I went to the country. Father decided not to join us and stayed in our apartment in Vienna. One day, the doorbell rang. Father, in his nightgown, tried to see who was at the door. He peeked out, but did not see anyone so he ventured out further. The door slammed and there he was in his knee-length white nightgown in the hallway of the apartment building. Panicked, he rang my grandfather's doorbell. Grandfather's new maid looked out, observed a man in a nightgown, screamed and did not let him in. I cannot remember how that story ended.

There was a similar incident in Vienna soon afterward that attracted the attention of Vienna newspapers because of the court case that followed.

A foreign student, who spoke very little German, rented a room in an apartment. The apartment owner was out of town and the student was taking a bath. Suddenly he heard the doorbell ring. He hopped out of the tub, which was still filling, made himself somewhat decent with a towel and opened the door. He put his hand out expecting the mailman. But there was no letter or mailman. He peeked out, the door slammed and there he was almost naked, barely covered by a towel, in the hallway of the apartment building with the water in the bathroom still running. He ran down to the concierge to report what had happened, but she had never seen him before and did not understand his agitated, fractured German and his pleas to turn off the water. All she saw was a more or less naked stranger and called the police. They threw him in jail for being disorderly or for indecent exposure, I do not remember which. They, in turn, did not understand his plea to turn off the water. He probably was an American or Englishman. Someone at the police station may have understood Serbo-Croatian, Czech or even Hungarian, but English!

The reason why this story appeared in the Viennese papers was that the poor student was sued for water damage in the apartment he rented and in the apartment below. He won his case. He had not been disorderly. He had tried to prevent the damages. An interpreter had been found. There was justice in Austria prior to March 1938.

In the autumn of 1928 a private tutor, a very nice young woman, was hired by my parents. Now I was tutored alone, no more school friends or classroom.

Soon I became very sick with diphtheria and missed weeks of instruction. I was nursed by my mother. So was Lily who also came down with that dreaded disease. She shared my room to make it easier for mother to nurse both of us. Lily tried to frighten me by making some awful sounds. I was scared, feverish, and very sick. A diphtheria vaccine had just been discovered and mother got the injection. My sister Hedy, Father and the maid had to move out. Diphtheria was a very dangerous disease and one had to be kept in complete isolation. Signs were posted outside the houses where victims of the epidemic lived. After the illness, houses had to be completely disinfected and everything (books, towels, toys, clothing) touched by the patient had to be burned. It took me a long time to recover from that disease.

January and February 1929 were the coldest months ever experienced in Vienna. It was so cold that the Danube was totally frozen over and one could walk from one shore to the other. My teacher took me to the banks of the Danube where we witnessed people cutting holes in the frozen river to swim in the icy waters. They belonged to the health club "Verkühle Dich Täglich" (Catch a Cold Daily). I remember that incident to this day. No more coal could be taken to Vienna by train—the railroads were totally frozen and damaged by the snow and ice. My grandfather had bought a little petrol stove and we assembled around it in his salon.

In the spring, I was running through our apartment, rounded a corner and fell. A terrible pain pierced my side. My appendix had burst and I needed emergency surgery. I was operated on that night in the same hospital where I saw the light of day. Lovely gentle nuns were my nurses. I remember my grandfather bringing spring flowers when he came to visit me. After my appendix operation my appetite increased, I ceased having all those miserable sore throats and infections, and became quite a healthy youngster.

The summer of 1929 was spent at a summer resort, Goesing. We went there and to Eisenstadt for several years. Goesing had a lovely big hotel. We saw the same people every year. Since Goesing was not far from Vienna, father was able to visit us on weekends. One day he came with his usual spats, cane and hat and we set out for a walk followed by my mother, friends and relatives. I carried his walking stick and used it as such. Suddenly, I screamed and then everyone else screamed. I had managed to stick the cane into a nest of wasps and we were all stung by the enraged insects. I had twelve stings over my body. We had to leave the stick where I dropped it. We took a path back that was slightly elevated and saw a little barefoot peasant boy approach the area where I had dropped the cane. We yelled at him to stay away from that place, but to no avail. He tried to retrieve the stick. I never heard a child scream as this poor little boy did when the wasps vented their fury on him.

A few weeks later, when we were still in Goesing a telegram arrived one day. Usually, telegrams meant bad news and so did this one. My mother was informed that my grandfather Braun had died of a sudden heart attack. He collapsed tying his shoelaces. My mother, who loved her Father dearly, was heartbroken. She wore black mourning clothes and a veil for an entire year. With her father's death, her moral support was gone and there were difficult changes to come in her life.

She inherited a third of her father's brewery shares. Uncle Kurt and Uncle Fritz inherited the other two-thirds. They were all rather wealthy now. Uncle Kurt was the new director at the brewery and lived in grandfather's house in Uherske Hradiste. Uncle Fritz, a chemist, was the brewer. We visited my uncles often and stayed with the Kurt Brauns in Uherske Hradiste. I became very friendly with my cousins Herta and Ernst. In later years, they attended a school in Vienna and stayed with us during the school year. Gretl Braun, Kurt's wife, and my mother were great friends.

We also spent vacations with Uncle Fritz, his wife Louise and my sick cousin Susi. They lived next to the brewery in Jarosov. The brewery was very modern for those days. A malt factory and bottling plant were attached. Uncle Fritz had to make his rounds in the early evening and I loved it when he took me along. Every time, we encountered a big toad sitting in the same place.

Jarosov was just a little Czech village—one road with houses on each side. Most of the villagers were employed by the brewery. They were given beer to take home in little pitchers at lunch and in the evening. At dusk, the cows and geese were driven home through the village street.

On Sundays, the village would burst into color. The peasants wore gorgeous colorful costumes. The boys wore embroidered white or cream-colored shirts, tight pants, high boots and little hats. The girls wore wonderful outfits: big headdresses embroidered in many colors; blouses with huge pleated, starched white sleeves ending in tight fitting lace and embroidery around the elbow; short embroidered colorful vests; and tight-fitting high red boots. Their skirts were above the knees. Actually, they were white aprons that were tied alternately to the back and to the front. They wore a short dark skirt over these and then a beautifully embroidered apron over all those many layered aprons. Each village had its own color scheme and embroidery design. At Easter, the villagers painted Easter eggs in the most intricate designs. At weddings, the young couple had to dance from one end of the village to the other in a fast gallop.

Uncle Fritz had a large library, including some rather dirty books that I discovered. I would look at the pictures in secret corners of the house. Uncle Fritz was my very favorite relative, gentle and sweet, with a funny sense of humor. He was a diabetic and had to give himself insulin injections everyday. He dearly loved his sick little daughter, Susi, and suffered with her. There was a tennis court attached to the house. My sister and I had a lot of fun playing there with some of the brewery office employees, after we emigrated to Czechoslovakia from Austria.

In the fall of 1929 I took my gymnasium entrance examinations.[8] I remember the little boy who was sitting next to me who was so busy trying to shield his answers to the questions from me. Actually, I had no intention of copying from him. His name was Klimt and he was the son, grandson or nephew of the famous Austrian painter Gustav Klimt.

I passed the exam and my gymnasium career started. This was my first public school in a rather rough area, but it was the only classical gymnasium (where Latin and Greek were taught). Since my father had had a classical education, he planned one for me, too.

There were mostly wild boys pummeling each other at every break. I was scared and bewildered after having spent my first school years in a rather pampered atmosphere. Besides Klimt and my best friend, Sylvia Grimm, there were no other Jewish children and only two or three other girls. After all the private schooling I had had up to then, I was terrified of my new classmates as I was

---

[8] In continental Europe (especially Germany), a gymnasium was a classical preparatory school to the universities.

painfully shy and lacked self-confidence. This was a very difficult time for me, and my father did not make it any easier. He attempted to teach me Latin and math in the same way he had done with the piano—and with similar results. I hated the school and father's tutoring. I was afraid of the wild boys.

Soon I would be able to leave all this behind. My parents were planning a divorce and the benefit to me was that father would lose interest in my education and mother would soon be able to enroll me in a fine, progressive, private girls' school, "Schwarzwald." The owner and director of the school was Dr. Eugenie Schwarzwald, a kind, educated and understanding woman.

MOTHER AND FATHER

My mother, Margarethe Back (Grete or Gretl to her friends), was a tall, good looking, very elegant woman with dark hair and dark eyes. She was nice and kind and highly educated. She came from a very good old family. She was raised in Uherske Hradiste, a small provincial town in Moravia when Moravia was part of the Austro-Hungarian monarchy. Now, it is in Czechoslovakian territory.

Mother was not college educated, but she received an extraordinarily fine education from governesses and tutors. She read a great deal and developed a great interest in art and music. She was also a fine pianist. I remember her playing the piano—Beethoven sonatas, Chopin, Caesar Frank—for hours when I was a child. When I was a teenager, she took me to museums, exhibitions, concerts, theater and the Opera House in Vienna.

She had a wonderful sense of humor. She could laugh herself sick over things that seemed funny to her. When we were little children we would crawl into her bed on Sunday mornings and she would read *The Adventures of the Good Soldier Schweik* to us. She would laugh so much that tears would roll down her cheeks. I am not sure how much we understood, but we got the idea that the book was very funny.

She could laugh and laugh but, unfortunately, her life was not all laughs. The death of her favorite brother Ernst in World War I was a terrible loss for her. She always told the story of how she dreamed one night in

1915 that she heard her father arrive in a taxi, slam the door, run up the stairs, ring the doorbell and burst into tears telling her that Ernst had been killed. She was about to tell her mother of her dream when a taxi drove up and her father slammed the taxi door and ran up the stairs. Her dream had been prophetic. My mother was heartbroken. Uncle Ernst's little terrier, Nicki, became our playmate and we all loved him dearly.

My mother was quite sentimental, and took her mother's, and later her beloved father's, deaths extremely hard. She was in deep mourning for a whole year for each of her parents. My father's unfaithfulness, his betrayal, his greed and the endless divorce procedures, which started soon after my grandfather died in 1929 and lasted until 1936, were devastating to her and very, very hard on me. My mother was totally obsessed by the divorce and I was drawn into all the sordid details as a young child.

Many years later, after my parents' divorce, my mother's first love, Schonsky, reappeared in her life and wanted to marry her again. By then, he was enormously wealthy. This time, I was totally opposed to the marriage. Schonsky was a rascal and had attempted to seduce my sister and one of my girlfriends. Later, I had regrets that I talked my mother out of marrying him. He had a Yugoslavian passport and it may have saved my mother's life, but he would have made her very unhappy.

My mother was in her middle twenties when World War I broke out. Having been denied the opportunity to marry Schonsky she married my father, perhaps on the rebound. My father had been wounded on Austria's eastern front and they met again when he was convalescing in Vienna. They were married at the military synagogue and everybody who remembered the ceremony recalled that she laughed and giggled throughout the service. Had she been able to foresee the future, she would not have laughed and rejoiced so much. Her marriage caused her pain, shame and heartache and was a total disaster. But, on that day in 1917, my mother was happy.

My father's most outstanding qualities were his good looks and his charm—not his character, nor his wisdom nor his kindness—but his looks. He never passed a mirror without looking into it. He always wore spats. Outdoors, he always wore a hat and had a walking stick with him.

He was born in 1884 and died in 1957. His name was Dr. Emmerich Back. He was quite musical and played the violin beautifully. My parents often played duets. There were chamber music evenings in our home when I was a child. I have wonderful memories of standing behind doors listening to them.

My father claimed to be a descendent of the great Jewish philosopher and advisor to Ferdinand and Isabella, Don Abravanel de Vega. Abravanel de Vega had to leave Spain in 1492, went to Sicily and later to Corsica. The Back family name is derived from the initials B.A.K.—Ben Abravanel Kodauschim, son of the holy Abravanel. My father legally adopted the last part of the name and was later known as Dr. Emmerich Back-Vega. My half-brother is Peter Back-Vega.

I do not know how my father obtained a law degree. According to the stories I heard as a child, he was kicked out of several high schools in Vienna and some provincial towns in Austria. He ended up going to school in Uherske Hradiste, where my mother grew up. They met on a skating rink when they were teenagers.

Somewhere along the line, my father received a classical education and used to quote pages and pages of the Iliad and Odyssey to me in Greek. How correctly, I could not judge; but I was very impressed. He was usually very moved by his own performance and had tears in his eyes at the end of his recitals. He knew Latin well and also mathematics. For that I can vouch, because after the initial disappointment that I was not a boy to carry on the family name, he drilled me in Latin and mathematics once I reached gymnasium age. It was a painful and frustrating experience.

Latin and my father's constant admonitions at age 10 were a nightmare for me. Latin was dropped as soon as he left us. However, the two years of Latin benefited me in the future. They gave me a sufficient foundation to guess at unknown English words on U.S. Civil Service tests. And, once settled in America, I was able to work for the Civil Service and earn a living.

My father always lived beyond his means and was unable to be faithful. My mother's dowry was invested by my patriotic grandfather and father in Austrian War Bonds, which had no value after the lost war. To my father's great disappointment, my grandfather had refused to take him into the family brewery. He started all kinds of business ventures but succeeded in none. He owned a bank and, in later years, a zinc and tin mine in Carinthia, Austria. He never practiced law. I suspect that he did not pass the bar.

He had good ideas but the time and place were always wrong. In America, he would have been a millionaire. He invested twice in oil. The first time it happened in Ploesti at the end of World War I—his business partner swindled him out of his share. The second time he invested in oil in Austria, but the Nazis took over. Nevertheless, my father had a capacity to live well.

He was a great Austrian patriot and a monarchist. He was severely wounded during World War I on the Russian front and carried the bullet that had been removed from his arm on his watch chain. He had it dipped in gold and it looked very pretty. He was always telling us that he had seen Emperor Franz Josef on the parade grounds. As a child, I had visions of the old Emperor picking up my poor wounded father and helping him. It could not have been the case, but I believe it was my father's proudest moment to have seen the Emperor at close range.

He was quite artistic, and besides being a violinist, he painted well and sculpted. After my parents married, and while my father was still recuperating from his wounds, they were stationed in a small Polish town. While there, he sculpted a statue of a warrior that later stood in the main square. He was very proud of this sculpture but I am quite convinced that it was removed as soon as Austrian troops left the territory they lost. My father probably should have stuck to art rather than to business and banking.

At Vienna University he belonged to several fighting fraternities. He was scarred by saber cuts which apparently was the ultimate honor and a source of great pride. He had fought several saber duels—any small provocation was grounds for such a fight. I have several letters written by my father about his duels.

THE DIVORCE

In early 1930 when we were in Uherske Hradiste, my mother received a letter from a lawyer. Father wanted a divorce and my mother's inheritance. All kinds of false claims were made by him—how he provided for my grandfather (who was an extremely well-to-do and generous man), how he was cheated out of a dowry and how he had not been taken into the family business.

Mother was terribly shocked that this should happen to her. A divorce! She did not suspect that Father was having an affair with Lily our cook, but all of Vienna knew. Father had been seen with Lily for the last few years but no one ever told mother. That blow came later. In the meantime, we returned to Vienna. There were terrible fights between my parents. Lily was the go-between, telling mother what father had said, and telling Father what mother had said. I found her listening behind doors.

Mother had a terrible time getting father out of our home. Although he wanted a divorce, he did not want to leave the comforts of her beautiful apartment on Weyrgasse. It adjoined our former apartment, but the arrangement of the rooms was more beautiful. When all the doors were open, one could see from one room to the next.

My father settled in the dining room and would not move. One day he fell asleep on the banks of the Danube where he was sunbathing and returned with a terrible sunstroke and high fever. mother had to nurse him. These were horrible times—fights, scenes, accusations, my mother crying and even attempted suicide. Eventually my father moved out. Lily had moved out earlier. My mother was mortified by the articles that started appearing in the Vienna press about my father and the divorce.

As upset as I was, there was a benefit for me in all this. mother took me out of that awful school environment even before the school year was over. I had been unhappy and scared at school, and now I did not have to live up to Father's expectations.

Most of my mother's cousins had attended Schwarzwald in Vienna, the private girls' gymnasium. I was enrolled there, but since I had had Latin before, I had to catch up on my English. At that time, I had a French governess, Madame Knopfmacher, who spoke excellent English. She and I were dispatched to Eisenstadt for the summer and she taught me English. It was decided that since I had missed so much school because of my various illnesses, it would be best to repeat the class I did not complete. During that summer in 1932 when we were in Eisenstadt, my great-grandmother Wolf died and all the family came to pay their respects.

From then on a much happier school time started for me. No more drilling by my father, no more wild boys. Julia, my relative and companion from first grade, was also at Schwarzwald with me. I lived rather far from the school and was given pocket money to use either for the bus or for "goodies." I usually used the bus, but when I was late and the bus had left, I ran all the way to school, then had to run up six flights of stairs. There were elevators of course, but by then there was no time to stand in line to wait for them. Julia was picked up by a chauffeur every day and sometimes I rode home with her. At the new school I had many friends and a lot of fun.

School was not so hard anymore and I was quite good in several subjects.

In the meantime, my parents were battling it out in the courts. My mother always won and Father would take the case to the next higher court and appealed every decision. Things dragged on. He did not pay child support or alimony and my mother had her revenge by having his furniture auctioned off. Once, before a court appearance, my Father kidnapped Hedy from the public school she attended. My mother was frantic. She suspected that he had taken her to Rodaun where my grandmother spent her summers. A relative of my mother's was sent to spy for her. There was Hedy with my Grandmother Back. Father called mother because he wanted some clothes for Hedy, but he would not disclose where she was. mother suggested he provide the clothes himself. The lawyer had advised mother not to panic, that Father used Hedy only to blackmail her. A day after my father's unsuccessful court appearance Hedy was returned home. I almost died of jealousy because it was Hedy who had been kidnapped and not I. Did my father love me less?

There was one more similar incident. Father did not pay for our upkeep so he was not allowed to see us—part of mother's revenge. However, one day a meeting between Father and us was arranged through the lawyers. Our governess Ami took us to see him in a *Konditorei* (a pastry shop). Suddenly, Ami realized that he wanted to take Hedy home with him. She slipped out and called mother. mother appeared soon afterward in a taxi accompanied by her lawyer and a policeman. We all had to go to the nearest police station. My mother and father walked in front, each pulling Hedy's arms; the policeman walked with them. I walked behind with the lawyer and Ami. I was crying bitterly from embarrassment and jealousy. Once again Father wanted to take Hedy and not me. Poor, poor me!

Things became worse. So much was written in the papers about my parents' divorce that one day Dr. Schwarzwald, the school principal, called me to her office and promised that she would protect me if children made fun of me or were unkind to me. I did not take her up on her offer. I did not need to. That was the time when mother's aunts, the many Wolf sisters, were very kind to me and I went to see them often to find solace.

The publicity in the papers was very embarrassing to my uncles. The family was well known and respected and they feared an adverse effect on their business. Were they really afraid that people in Czechoslovakia would drink less of our beer? Maybe they were trying to protect us. In any case, it was decided that my mother should pacify my Father by giving him money. To do this, mother sold some of her shares in the family brewery (which left her with a smaller income). The shares were bought by my uncles. At the same time, it became more difficult to transfer money from Czechoslovakia to Austria and things became financially harder for us. mother rearranged the large apartment and rented out two rooms. We then had only one live-in maid, a cleaning woman, a laundress and a woman to do the ironing.

Things at school went smoothly, but mother's obsession with the endless divorce continued. She could not talk about anything else or think about anything else. Her world now was "the divorce." When guests would arrive, I would run to meet them and beg them to change the subject of conversation. Eventually, she showed interest in other things again.

In 1936, the divorce was final and Father married Lily. He still refused to pay child support and court appearances continued. But things eased off for us. I had started going to a dancing school (ballroom dancing at Ellmayer's), went skating almost daily in winter and did a lot of skiing. We went swimming in summer and all kinds of young boys attached themselves to me and soon I had a great romance.

Father had Lily and money; and Lily was called Frau Doctor Back, like my mother. She had some talent as a painter and my Father had her trained at the Academy of Arts in Vienna. My Father and his brothers, Richard and Oscar, were avid collectors of paintings. Somehow, my Father increased his collection. He overvalued his paintings. Oscar had a few first-class paintings—a Teniers, and a Hedda, and others.

My Father had always been an extremely vain man. His suits were made by the best tailor in Vienna. Since my mother was not there to pay his debts to tailors and other creditors, he ran afoul of the various bill collectors. This, too, was written about in the Vienna papers. He was a selfish man, concerned only with himself, and we were the ones who had to suffer.

JANCSI—MY FIRST LOVE

This is hard for me to write. I cannot help thinking of what might have been, what could have been and what never was.

My mother's oldest cousin, Rosa, was married to an Hungarian and lived in Budapest. She often came to Vienna to visit her family. In 1933, she came to Vienna and invited me to travel with her to Budapest and stay with her for some time. We took a Danube steamer down the river to Budapest. We passed Carnuntum, the old Roman fortification along the Danube, and Bratislava, the capital of Slovakia, which seemed most attractive from the boat landing. There was a large beautiful building (perhaps a castle) and a large square opposite the landing with hills in the background. We moved on, watching the riverbed become wider and wider. At one point it suddenly curves southward. The banks are totally flat and the landscape is not particularly attractive.

We arrived in Budapest late in the evening. The city was illuminated beautifully. The Parliament building and a famous landmark in Budapest, the Fischerbastei, the Hotel Gellert, and some of the bridges were illuminated as if for a special occasion. Perhaps it was in honor of my arrival and my first love—a love that was not to be, that was thwarted by age (too young), by immaturity, by circumstances, and by world history (the war).

Budapest is a very lovely city divided by the huge river that dominates it. Pest is built on a plain; Buda is built on terraced hills where there are still mementos from the Turkish domination of the Magyar city. I cannot remember how long I stayed in Budapest. It seemed forever and yet, it was not long enough.

The evening after our arrival, Rosa took me to a little summer cottage in the hills of Buda. It belonged to her husband's relatives. The atmosphere was very sedate, a little stiff and quiet, but young people were expected after a day of boating on the Danube. Soon they arrived—charming, noisy Hungarian boys and girls. And there was Jancsi—handsome as a young god, tall, enchanting. He was just 18, had matriculated recently and was enrolled at the university. I do not think he realized how attractive he was. He was very natural. He spoke a very funny German, probably an equally funny Italian and French, all with a strong Hungarian accent.

It was St. Stephan's day, the day of the patron saint of Hungary. There were fireworks along the Danube illuminating the lovely city. Jancsi simply took my hand, we climbed a hill, sat on the grass and watched the fireworks. I cannot remember what happened with the other young people. We were alone on the hill. After that evening, and for the rest of my stay in Budapest, we were inseparable. He showed me Budapest and the lovely rose garden on St. Margaret's Island. We swam in the pool at the elegant Gellert Hotel and in public swimming pools. We went rowing with his friends and cousins on the Danube. At night we went to gypsy taverns. We took a cruise up the Danube. We went dancing, we flirted—we were in love. It was wonderfully romantic. Then I had to return to Vienna and school.

Jancsi and I corresponded. He sent me flowers. Crushed chocolate bonbons arrived in letters. He phoned me. It was pure, heavenly love. I told Liesl, my best friend, about Jancsi. Liesl was horrified—her friend having a very serious romance at fifteen! (She probably had not experienced romance yet.) She was concerned about my virtue and morals.

Liesl had a very strong influence on me. She was afraid we might go too far. I did not even know what "going too far" meant. I was too innocent. And how far could we go while Jancsi was in Budapest and I was in Vienna! In any case, I had to promise Liesl that I would write to him and break it off. And, I, an idiot, did what I had promised her. I wrote Jancsi that we were too young and should stop what was by now a friendship through the mail. He replied that he was glad that I had written that letter because he, too, had the same thought and was about to write a similar letter. And that was that, other than exchanging occasional greeting cards.

When I was seventeen or eighteen I received a telephone call. Jancsi was in Vienna and wanted to see me. By then I had another entanglement, Herbert. I remembered my promise to Liesl; but here was Jancsi in Vienna. What was I to do? I took Hedy with me to meet Jancsi. We had not seen each other for several years. Hedy looked very much like me and I hoped that Jancsi would mistake her for me. (Only an immature teenager could come up with such an idea.) Jancsi, of course, knew me at once and I dropped Herbert like a hot potato. I am sure he never knew why.

This time, I was Jancsi's tour guide through Vienna, Schoenbrunn, St. Stephan's Cathedral, the Prater, etc. We went dancing, to a costume ball, to the Opera. We sat in a Viennese park at dusk and watched the gas lamps being lit. There was the same magic and romance. He was a law student by then and still handsome and charming. Within a few weeks he had to return home to Budapest.

Again there were letters, flowers, crushed chocolates in letters, and telephone calls. We met in little towns between Budapest and Vienna, sometimes in Hungary, sometimes in Austria for a day. It was all very harmless.

Once, we met in a little town in Hungary. We went to a small farm, ordered chicken for lunch and went for a walk while the meal was being prepared. Suddenly we heard a terrific turmoil. It was the poor chicken putting up its last struggle. Soon there was chicken paprika on the table. But I had little stomach for it after hearing the chicken giving up its soul.

I saw Jancsi again in Budapest when I stayed with Rosa at Christmas time 1936. He was going through very hard times. His father, a well-known gynecologist in Budapest, was very ill. Jancsi was in law school and had to work, in addition to attending lectures and studying. He worked in a bank to help his mother financially. He was under great emotional strain.

When I was back in Vienna, his letters became rarer and rarer. During the time of our romance, I did not date anyone else and did not go out socially, to my mother's great dismay, but waited from letter to letter, from call to call. During the 1937-38 ball season I started to go out again to dances and balls. Then came the Nazis and all that came to an abrupt halt. We left Vienna and emigrated to Czechoslovakia.

Jancsi's father died after a long illness and Jancsi received his law degree. We never saw each other again.

VACATIONS

School vacations in Austria were much shorter than they were in the United States, yet long enough to do all kinds of interesting things. At Christmas, we often went skiing in the Alps. Part of summer vacation was always spent in Eisenstadt, the rest of the time was spent in the mountains along lakes or the seashore.

Vienna was very hot and humid in summer. The asphalt became soft and soggy from the heat; the nights were unbearable. The houses radiated heat and whoever could tried to escape. There was no air conditioning and, in private homes, it does not exist to this day.

Summer 1934

In 1934 I was sent to a summer camp in Rimini-Miramare near Riccione in Italy. It was run by a mother and her daughters. We went by train from Vienna and travelled for many hours. When I looked out of the window at dawn, we were on a long viaduct extending over the ocean connecting the mainland to Venice. This was my first glimpse of the ocean—fishing boats on the smooth surface of the water. The sea shimmered and gleamed in the light of the rising sun. In a distance were the towers and cupolas of Venice—an unforgettable scene. The train stopped in Venice, but we did not get out. We returned to Mestre, the station at the other end of the viaduct, and continued our trip to Rimini-Miramare.

It was a wonderful summer. The house we stayed in was on the beach. There were boys and girls my age and we made unforgettable excursions into the surrounding areas. We went to San Marino, a fascinating tiny republic in the Kingdom of Italy. For a time after the war it became a small communist enclave in the Republic of Italy. The landscape, between the ocean and the rock the little country is situated on, is totally flat and then the perpendicular rock rises several hundred feet. The mountain has three peaks with a castle on each peak and an ancient wall connecting the castles. There were small, medieval houses, and no traffic. One soldier defended the little country, one policeman kept order, and there was only one prisoner when I was there. Very rare postage stamps are minted there. We had a breathtaking view of the Adriatic. I remember feeling very insignificant looking down the steep precipice and observing a football game below, played by what appeared to be very active ants.

Another excursion took us to Ravenna, one of the rare treasures of the world. It was the city of the Emperor Justinian and the capital of the East Roman Empire for many centuries. The mosaics inside the churches are simply magnificent, some of the finest in the world. The exteriors of the buildings seem insignificant but the interiors of the churches, the baptistery and the mausoleum of Galla Placidia are decorated with spectacular gold leaf interspersed with other colored precious stones. They made an unforgettable impression on me. The buildings are from the Byzantine period. The most beautiful churches are St. Appolinare Nuovo, it contains magnificent mosaics, and St. Appolinare in Classe, which depicts Christ with a little lamb on a gold and blue mosaic background. San Vitale is the most spectacular of the churches. This church is from the sixth century, octagonal in shape and contains the large mosaic pictures of Justinian, his attendants and his Empress Theodora with her court.

We stood at Dante's tomb. But the deepest impression on me was made by the tomb of Galla Placidia, a small octagonal room covered with the loveliest mosaics and windows of precious stones. The light was refracted through those windows into a multitude of colors. Galla Placidia had been a slave, became an empress and, I believe, became a slave again. She was entombed in that magnificent mausoleum. Her corpse was supposed to have sat on a throne in imperial splendor for centuries until a child entered with a candle and all fell to dust.

We saw Rimini and Francesca da Rimini's palace and crossed the Rubicon where Caesar spoke the famous words: "Alea jacta est" (the die is cast).

In Rimini Miramare, we were housed in a building just a few feet away from the shore. We went swimming along the coast early in the morning. The water was so clear and blue we could see little shells and starfish at the bottom of the ocean bed. We would swim along the beach, our bathing suits slung around our necks. After a long swim, we would hurry home, return to bed and later join the rest of the group for breakfast.

One day, we observed Mussolini and his son Bruno at the opening of a summer home for poor children from Bologna. The little boys wore blue bathing suits and the girls wore pink. All wore little hats. Mussolini stood on top of the roof with his son next to him. He made a long speech. After the speech, all the children threw their hats into the air and sang fascist songs. The children had a good time, but were terribly regimented and treated like little soldiers. They went swimming, accompanied by whistle blows, came out of the water, went to eat, and to play, all to the tune of the whistle. The older boys, maybe twelve years old, drilled with rifles. This was Mussolini's fascist Italy.

This was the summer when Engelbert Dollfuss, the Austrian chancellor, was assassinated by Nazi thugs. Dollfuss had signed a pact with Mussolini, and Mussolini amassed his troops on the Brenner pass. This deterred Hitler from marching into Austria at that time.

We often walked to Riccione, the lovely Adriatic resort, close to Rimini Miramare. One evening we went dancing. A very handsome Italian asked me for every dance and walked me home along the shore. I was in a blue evening gown. The next day he came to see me at the beach. But what a disappointment—my handsome Italian was covered with pockmarks. I had not noticed the night before when we were bathed in candlelight.

In the last days of my stay in Rimini Miramare, I became terribly ill with paratyphoid and collapsed in the bathroom, too weak to get up. I managed to crawl back to the room on my hands and knees to the astonishment of my roommates. I recovered in time for a short visit to Venice on the way home to Vienna. Once at home I had a relapse and was terribly sick for weeks. Mother nursed me back to health.

Summer 1935

My sister was an excellent swimmer. If the 1936 Olympics had not been held in Berlin, she would have been on the Austrian Olympic team. In 1935 there were swim meets in Mondsee, and arrangements for Hedy and me had been made at a summer camp. My sister and I spent a lovely vacation along the shores of the charming

Mondsee—one of the most beautiful lakes of the Salzkammergut. Besides my sister, and another girl and myself, there were no other campers. But there was a lot of staff. An old Austrian major guided us on wonderful hikes up and down the mountains. He found marvelous spots with magnificent views, We were guided by his compass and his maps. After the Nazi takeover, I bumped into him on the streets of Vienna. He asked me what we were going to do and I told him that we planned to go to England eventually. The sweet man broke into tears and expressed his sorrow on how everything had turned out, wished me luck and said farewell.

Hedy and I often traveled to Salzburg from Mondsee, and once sat in a tree watching a performance of Goethe's *Faust* in an open air amphitheater there. It was a Max Reinhardt production—no stage, no curtains, but the sets were arranged for the different scenes. Scenes where the action took place were picked up by spotlights. We also saw Reinhard's production of Jedermann in front of the Cathedral. The stage was made up of wooden boards and the whole city participated in the play. The sun stood high in the sky when the play began. All the bells of the many churches in the city rang. "Death" appeared in the window of the Cathedral's belfry, voices sounded from all the mountains, and when Jedermann died, the sun set and the stage was bathed in darkness. Unforgettable!

I fell in love with enchanting Salzburg, nestled among the lower reaches of the Alps. It was a beautiful city bustling with excitement during the festivals. On a mountain high above the town is the Hohenfeste, the Archbishop's ancient fortification. Just below the rocky mountain is peaceful, lovely St. Peter's cemetery. Early Christians had chiseled tiny churches into the rock. There are several of these ancient Christian Churches above the cemetery, each one a little bigger than the preceding one. As Christianity developed and was accepted among the original pagan population, the churches became bigger and bolder. There are several of these ancient churches above the ancient graves. Near the entrance to the cemetery are seven crosses with another cross several feet away. These are the graves of a man and the seven wives he tickled to death!

I will never forget being in a rowboat on Mondsee (Moon Lake) with the reflection of the moon receding in the dark waters. The landscape was bathed in the moon's pale light, and on the shore a radio was playing Beethoven's Moonlight Sonata. Sheer bliss.

In the evening, we often went dancing. Once a young boy who had asked me to dance made anti-Semitic remarks. I told him I was Jewish but he kept coming back to ask me for more dances. I refused him, of course. I saw him later on the streets of Vienna. He always tipped his hat in a greeting, but I looked away.

I learned to ride a bicycle in Mondsee but never got over the unsteady stage. There was a big castle in Mondsee. Two young sons of the castle's owner flirted with me. One day I dared to ride through the village and the two young men were sitting in an outdoor cafe. They looked at me. I became flustered, fell off the bicycle, hurt my knee and ran away leaving the bicycle to be picked up later by my roommate. The humiliation of it!

Summer 1936

Our summer vacation was spent in Bled. My mother, sister and I stayed in a hotel overlooking the charming lake of Bled in the mountains of Yugoslavia. The Yugoslavian royal family had their summer palace along the lake's shore and we frequently saw them there and at tennis tournaments. There was a small island in the lake and I often swam there. It was a lovely, peaceful, uneventful summer vacation. There was not a ripple on the surface of the water.

Summer 1937

I graduated from the gymnasium in 1937 and my mother's brother, Kurt, invited me to spend my summer vacation with my Aunt Gretl and my cousins Herta and Ernst in Laurana, Italy. Laurana was situated on a bay and one could see the Dalmatian coast of Yugoslavia in the distance. The border between Italy and Yugoslavia was in Fiume, sometimes dividing not only the town but even a room in a home into an Italian and a Yugoslavian section.

The coast is very rocky and quite wild there. Walking at night, we saw glowing fish hiding in the little bays and inlets. Some rocks were some distance from the shore. We would swim out to the rocks and sometimes we saw lobsters perching on them. We observed an elderly woman swimming in a bathing suit that covered her from head to toe with a strand of pearls around her neck. My cousins and I were very amused by her appearance and not very discreet about hiding our merriment. Later we were told that the lady was the former queen of Bulgaria.

We took a boat tour to one of the islands along the coast. It was flat, dry and totally medieval. For centuries it was occupied by robber barons who had been a peril to shipping vessels along the coast. That summer vacation was not a totally happy one for me. I was observing the happy family life of my Aunt and Uncle and cousins. I never knew that type of family devotion. Having been without a father since 1930 had been very hard for me and I felt jealous, unhappy and envious.

At the end of our Italian vacation, we took a boat trip from Fiume to beautiful Venice. We stopped at Pola and saw the spectacular Roman amphitheater facing the harbor.

On the boat an elderly man, who was, perhaps, forty years old, and an acquaintance of my uncle and aunt, whispered to me that he would visit me in my cabin at night. I was not sure whether he was joking or would really appear there. I was petrified and wanted to be prepared, but could not lock the cabin. What could I do to defend myself? I asked the steward for a large pitcher of water and there I was, sitting all night long in my cabin, ready for the intruder who never came.

Venice was glorious—trips in gondolas, visits to the Palace of the Doges, to churches, to museums. There was a remarkable Tintoretto exhibit that made an indelible impression on me. We saw the wonderful painting by Titian "The Ascension to Heaven" in the Frari church. We saw a funeral and wedding procession in gondolas. We went to the Lido and the highlight of it all was a visit to San Marco. High mass was being said with sunlight streaming through the stained glass windows, illuminating the golden robes of the clergy and the shining, colorful mosaics. It was a sight unforgettable to this day, more than fifty years later.

We stayed in a small hotel. The streets outside were so narrow we were able to observe two Italian girls across the street getting ready for the evening. It took them all day—with curlers in their hair and ironing dresses—to get ready. At night we saw them in the piazza. Their efforts paid off. They were gorgeous. Beautiful Venice—it is still very beautiful but so much more crowded than it was then.

I think back to these summers of my youth with nostalgia. They belong to an unretrievable world of yesterday. The year 1938 brought very bitter realities and heartaches; 1939 heralded in the war.

PRELUDE TO CATASTROPHE

1937 to March 1938

The divorce of my parents was finally behind us. It took years and years to dissolve this marriage. It caused my mother such heartache and such grief. I, too, was very badly affected and drawn into all this when I was very young. The disputes over alimony and child care payments no longer continued. Father had married our cook, and after he had attempted to kidnap Hedy for a second time, we were not allowed to see him. Life became quite placid and pleasant, something to be enjoyed, not to agonize over. Mother had recovered from the pain that had been inflicted upon her. My health was excellent now, and Jancsi a mere memory. I was young and having a very good time.

Early in the ball season of 1937, I attended a ball at the Schwarzenbergplatz. It caused me much anguish. I was so afraid I would not have enough dancing partners. No sooner did I arrive at the ball, accompanied by my mother, than red wine was spilled on my light blue evening gown. But I did not miss a dance and had a great time. I still remember the names of some of my partners. What became of them? Where did they go?

I went skating and skiing, and often on Sunday mornings walked on the Corso (the stretch of the Ringstrasse between Schwarzenbergplaz and the Opera) where all the young "in" people met. And I prepared for my graduation from the gymnasium. My major fields of interest were

English history (the Stuart Restoration), German literature and math.

The summer of 1937 was dreadfully hot. The days were too humid to study, but I was up almost every night doing so. The subject of the essay portion of the matriculation was a quotation by Goethe: "And what I am I owe to others." We had several hours to develop the theme. I remember writing what we are we owe to our genes and our environment and dragged up theoretical examples of identical twins developing in the same and different environments. I did well on this test and on my English test, but math was a disaster.

I was actually quite good in math and had prepared myself for the test. I had studied, and to make sure I would do well, I had mathematical formulas written inside my belt and on my thighs. But I let myself be waylaid by the wrong information left behind in the toilet. Of twenty-eight girls, twenty-six made the same mistake. The twenty-six failed the written part of the exam. It caused a terrific scandal. The Board of Education was outraged. It was decided that one had to perform over a certain grade on the oral test to overcome the failure. My maiden name started with a "B" and I was the first to prepare answers to very difficult questions on the blackboard. My professor, Dr. W., gave me eye signals. He was sitting with the other examiners in a semicircle. When I did well, he slowly closed his eyes. I passed and did not have to repeat the test in the fall. I had my lovely vacation in Italy with my Aunt, Uncle and two cousins and saw glorious Venice.

I had intended to study art history but decided on photography instead. The Nazis were in power in Germany and the reports about what was happening to German Jews were very disquieting. A doctorate in Art History would have taken four years and I realized that

I would not have that much time with the Nazis' threatening approach. Instead, I enrolled in the renowned Graphical Institute of Vienna where I learned the intricacies of photography, optics, chemistry, drawing and bookkeeping. I attended classes three afternoons a week. The practical aspects of portrait photography I later learned in a well-known portrait studio where I apprenticed.

My mother paid for my apprenticeship. It proved to have been a very good decision. I earned my living doing photography for many years, had wonderful experiences as a news photographer, met my husband, also a photographer, came to America with him, and still enjoy taking pictures of my grandchildren.

There was not enough time to go home for lunch on days I attended the Graphical Institute. On those days I ate at the home of a cousin of my grandfather. He had a fabulous picture collection, which was later sold in Australia for a lot of money. He and his wife had a beautiful apartment and were most kind, maybe too kind. Every time his wife left the room, Uncle felt it necessary to try to pinch and touch me. I dreaded my luncheons there. I did not know how to escape him. I did not dare to tell my mother that the old, venerated relative was not so respectable after all. All this ended in March 1938 anyway.

I was the only Jewish youngster in the class at the Graphical Institute and had more education than the other young people there who had become apprentices at age fourteen. I did enjoy the photography courses. On the long way home from school, I usually visited pastry shops where chestnut cream was a specialty.

Our financial situation deteriorated considerably due to two primary factors: mother sold many of her brewery shares leaving her with a smaller monthly income, and the trade barriers between Austria and Czechoslovakia made transfers of currency between the two countries virtually impossible. This situation did not worry me but forced mother to rent some rooms in our beautiful large apartment and do her own cooking.

The first boarder, Herr von Winternitz, was a lovely old man who had been very wealthy before World War I and a great friend of one of the archdukes. I visited him often. He entertained me with my favorite candies and stories of high society during the Austrian monarchy. I remember one story in particular of ladies of Vienna aristocracy doing a stint in Prague's bordellos.

I was very sad when he died suddenly. Years earlier, he had been run over by a car in Berlin. His stomach was lopsided—rather flat on one side and enormous on the other—as a consequence of the accident. Poor man. I missed him, his stories and the obvious pleasure my visits gave him.

After Herr von Winternitz, mother rented to an American whom I actually never met with his clothes on. But twice I found him swimming in our bathtub. (He had forgotten to lock the door.) It was the very bathtub in which he died of a stroke.

After that, mother rented to German refugees. Through them and the newspapers we knew pretty well what was happening in Germany. But life in Vienna was very nice in 1937, if one could only turn one's mind away from Nazi Germany, Hitler's tirades over the radio and the agitations of the local Nazis.

In the fall of 1937, my uncles tried to persuade my mother to move to Prague. Money transfers from Czechoslovakia were becoming harder and harder to accomplish. One actually had to smuggle money into Austria. The boarders were to provide for the day-to-day expenses. It was decided that mother and I would go to Prague to investigate life there.

I fell in love with the beautiful city. The first afternoon we walked through the streets of Prague, a number of young men whom I had never seen in my life greeted me on the street. When I was introduced to some people in a coffeehouse they were perplexed. Two young Prague society girls looked like identical twins. One was usually mistaken for the other—and now I came along resembling them. That accounted for my being greeted by total strangers.

I enjoyed my stay in Prague, but my mother did not like the city, the beautiful baroque capital of Czechoslovakia. The strange things that went on in our hotel, the Golden Goose, may have had something to do with mother's distaste. It seemed to only be inhabited by men. They were lurking in the corridors and in front of the hotel. In my innocence I did not know what it was all about. I just loved this enchanting city on the Moldau and was ready to give up Vienna for Prague.

The city has a lovely bridge across the river decorated with statues of saints. The bridge led from the more modern section to medieval Prague. Little streets wind their way upward toward the ancient castle on the hill, the Hradcany, and the old Cathedral. There is the street of the Alchemists, where the houses are not higher than a man standing upright. But the secret of making gold had eluded them all. One of the Holy Roman Emperors, Ottokar (1251-1278), had toiled with the alchemists and he, too, failed, as he had in other respects. One of my relatives gave me an unforgettable tour of ancient Prague. We started at the foot of the old city. We walked through small houses and apartments, climbed stairs, crossed gardens, but never any streets and suddenly found ourselves at Hradcany Castle.

I was enchanted by the prospect of living in Prague and hoped to move there immediately. Mother would not hear of it. We returned to Vienna, which soon was invaded by Germans. If only we had known.

I had developed a nice relationship with my mother by this time. We did many things together. She was a great music lover; and we attended concerts and the Opera together. We went to exhibitions and visited friends and relatives. I even persuaded her to come with me on an excursion into the Vienna woods. But that was not very successful because she wore high heels and could barely walk.

New Year's eve of 1937-38 I spent with my best friend Liesl (the one who had me write the "Dear John" letter to Jancsi), at the Opera. It was a traditional Viennese New Year's eve. We heard Johann Strauss' "Die Fledermaus" and Richard Tauber sang the part of one of the guests at Prince Orlovsky's party.

The year 1938 started very promisingly. If we could only forget the Germans next door and not listen to Hitler's interminable speeches and the agitations of the local Nazis.

The ball season got into full swing after January 6th. I attended many balls in palaces, clubs and in private homes. To the Gschnasfest, a ball given by Vienna artists, I wore a Czech peasant costume. My mother had it made for me using beautiful Czech embroidery she had collected. (I still have the costume.) I went to the ball with a large group of people, but at one point found myself in the car of a former admirer of mine. We were in the Prater. It was dawn and Rudy, a friend for years, was at my side. To this day, I do not know how we got away from the ball, how we got to the Prater and why. Unaccustomed to drinking, I probably had had one too many.

ANSCHLUSS AND EMIGRATION

For four weeks prior to the Anschluss (annexation) of Austria, there was a lot of unrest in Vienna, demonstrations in the streets, a lot of "Siegheiling" and "Heil Hitlering."[9] Police on horseback tried to disperse the crowds. I got caught up in the crowd several times on the way home from school or the studio. It was very frightening. I remember one day being at the movies and seeing the beautiful film, "How Green Was My Valley." It was very moving, but suddenly we heard all the brutal, rowdy noises outside. By the time the film was over quiet had been restored.

From 1933, Austria was no longer a democracy. Engelbert Dollfuss, the chancellor, a pint-size man in every respect, had suspended parliament, democracy, freedom of the press, freedom of assembly, and, to the chagrin of our German neighbors, imposed a 1000 Mark charge on every German intending to enter Austria. Dollfuss went against the Austrian Nazis but the Austrian socialists became his real target.

In 1933, Dollfuss dissolved all parties except his clerical-fascist "Fatherland Front." In 1934 when the socialists rose up in anger, he had the Fatherland Front troops shoot into the huge modern housing project for workers, the Karl Marx Hof. They used field artillery. The socialist leaders were supposed to have congregated there. We heard the bombardment for days. Access to the

[9] These were Nazi salutations.

Inner City had been cut off and one could not move from one part of the city to another. More than one thousand people were killed. In July 1934, Dollfuss was assassinated in the chancellery on Ballhausplatz. Nazis were responsible for the crime. Mussolini and Yugoslavia then concentrated their troops on the Brenner pass and prevented the Germans from taking over Austria.

Kurt von Schuschnigg became the new chancellor of Austria. Fascism was the order of the day and our neighbor was arming all the time. For years, Austrian and German Nazis agitated and demanded unification with Germany. There was unrest in the streets and many bombings of the beautiful city of my birth. On February 12, 1938, von Schuschnigg visited Hitler in Berchtesgarden. Hitler ranted and raved, and made terrible scenes. Von Schuschnigg had to make many concessions, such as releasing Nazis from prison, even some of Dollfuss' assassins, and appointing a Nazi as Minister of the Interior. When Nazis were released from prison, von Schuschnigg freed socialists, too.

On February 20, 1938, we were all glued to radio sets to listen to Hitler screaming and yelling. Our fate depended on that man. After February 12th, there was constant unrest in the city of Vienna.

On March 9th, von Schuschnigg suddenly asked for a plebiscite to be held on March 13th. He made overtures to Austrian social democrats, but by then it was too late. To avoid the outcome of a plebiscite, Hitler suddenly moved his armies against Austria.

We decided that we definitely had to be ready to leave at a moment's notice, and thus, needed to get our passports renewed. For weeks my sister and I tried through our lawyer to get father, our legal guardian, to sign our passports so we could leave if we had to. (In case the Nazis took over, one just needed a passport to get away.)

It took a court order to force him to sign them. On March 11, 1938 Hedy and I finally met him at the passport office in Breunerstrasse and he did sign. We now had our passports. I proceeded to the photo studio and later went on to the Graphical Institute.

We got the passports just in time. March 11th was the day the Nazis came to power, and without that passport Hedy and I could not have escaped. Fate?!

I was at the Graphical Institute that Friday, March 11th. On the way home from school, I could not get through the Inner City—it was cordoned off. Vienna's first district, the old city, is surrounded by a beautiful wide chestnut tree-lined street, the Ringstrasse, where the streetcars travel. It was easy to cordon off the Inner City where the government offices were located. Another wide street, the Gürtel (belt), runs parallel to the Ringstrasse. Traffic was diverted to the Gürtel, but the Gürtel was much further and it took me hours to get home. On the stretches I walked, there were crowds milling around me. Rumors were flying, but I did not really know what was going on.

When I arrived home, the husband of my private English teacher called. He was looking for his wife and advised us to turn on the radio. At that moment, von Schuschnigg was abdicating. His speech was very moving. His voice broke, and then Haydn's beautiful hymn, the Austrian anthem, was played. A few minutes later the same melody, with different words, the German anthem, played. Von Schuschnigg was arrested as soon as his speech ended.

This news only incited me to leave Austria immediately and go to Czechoslovakia, as long as the borders were still open. Leave everything behind, take the next train, just go. But now came the voice of reason—one had to weigh the events, one had to think, make plans, arrive at decisions. One could not be hasty. Things may not be as bad as they seemed. All this thinking and considering was wrong, of course. We should have gone then and there. The borders were still open; but the next day they were closed and one could not get away. Leaving was much more difficult and we could not rescue any of our belongings anyway.

The Nazis came in with a fury and vengeance. By the next day the whole city was decked out with Nazi flags. There were huge pictures of Hitler everywhere. All but the Jews wore Nazi badges and swastikas. The victims were easily recognizable. We had become the pariahs. Ugly Nazi slogans of Jewish blood streaming from knives were sung. Life had become awful. We knew we had to leave to save ourselves. But where would we go? What would we do? Mother's brothers wanted us to go to Czechoslovakia where mother was born and where my uncles had influence.

The German army moved into Austria on March 12th. By March 13th the annexation of Austria was completed. Hitler came for a short visit to Vienna on March 14th. Czechoslovakia was surrounded by Germany on three sides. That night I sat down and wrote to the only English woman I knew to help us to get to England. She was Romanian by birth, British by nationality and had been mother's tennis partner. The only way to get to England was as a domestic. Of course I wanted to go, but I had to wait in Czechoslovakia until the papers were ready. Our friend procured an au pair job for me and the necessary papers, but it took a long time, a whole year.

Hitler had actually bluffed. His armies were not ready to fight, but they poured into Austria, including Vienna and marched. The same planes flew over the city again and again. The same troops went around and around the Ringstrasse. We later learned that many of his panzers (tanks) had broken down on highways. Planes swooped low over the city releasing antisemitic propaganda pamphlets. We knew what was in store for us.

France and England did not call his bluff. France did nothing to help us. As usual, they were without a government. Britain made protestations. Mussolini stayed out of it. That was that. It was a fait accompli.

Austria did not exist any longer. It was now called Ostmark. Vienna, the beautiful old baroque city, was relegated to a place among many German cities. Seventy-nine thousand Viennese citizens were arrested within hours of the Anschluss as "unreliable."

An absolute orgy of cruelty, sadism, inhumanity, and chicanery followed. Hitler ordered a plebiscite for April 10. Guess who won by 99.75%? Vienna had a highly cultured, highly educated Jewish population. They now suffered untold humiliation. The Nazis gathered Jews to scrub floors in Nazi caserns with acid added to the water.[10] Girls were picked up to wash latrines. Jews had to scrub the streets of Vienna to the taunts of the gathered onlookers. Old bearded religious Jews were forced to run races to the derision of Nazi hordes. Pregnant women were gathered in the Prater also to run races to amuse their bestial onlookers.

Relatives of my mother, Professor Nobel and his wife, threw themselves out of a window when Nazis appeared at their door. Our friend, Ernst Heller, shot himself when they invaded his home. They tried to scare people out of their wits. They gathered part of a family in one part of an apartment and the rest in another, then they shot pistols into the air and pulled a rug from under them. The

---

[10] Caserns were barracks or some sort of lodging for soldiers in a garrison town.

people fell and their relatives thought that their loved ones were killed.

My father, we were told, was picked up by the Gestapo and held at the infamous Hotel Metropol. The father of my good friend and cousin Heidi was picked up by Nazis at random. They did not even know his name or who he was. These hoodlums entered the building where the Goldschmidts lived. They went from door to door, floor to floor, in search of Jews whom they could pick up and cart away.

The Goldschmidts lived on the top floor; they took Friedl with them and sent him to Dachau. Friedl Goldschmidt was a stout, harmless, lovely and kind man in his early fifties. A few days later, he was returned home in a coffin. The family was admonished not to open it. I went through that ordeal with Heidi and her family. I know how they suffered.

We all lived in fear and panic during those horrible times. My mother, sister and I lived in our apartment without men. Our maid was with us and she was extremely loyal. Male friends and relatives often came to our home to hide from the Nazi raids. They felt safer with us than in their own homes. Those were terrible times. Those who have not lived through them will never know how awful it was. I am aware that it became much worse later on.

One day, I walked home from the photo studio. I was dressed very simply, no makeup. I tried not to be noticed, to blend in. I avoided streets where Nazi headquarters were located, or where there were a lot of Nazi activities. It was shortly after the Anschluss. On the other side of the street walked an SA man and a fellow with an armband. (They did not all have their uniforms yet.) They walked in the opposite direction. Suddenly they crossed the street and blocked my path. Jews were easily recognizable as they did not wear any Nazi insignias.

They asked me briskly, "Are you Austrian?"

I answered, "Yes."

"Are you Jewish?"

I repeated, "Yes."

"Come with us."

One walked in front of me and the other behind me. I tried to be very nonchalant and not give them any cause for derision. I acted as if nothing was happening. I blew my nose and asked them if I could call my mother when we arrived wherever we were going as I was expected home for lunch. I got a brusque "Yes" as an answer.

Eventually we arrived at St. Stephan's Square, the main square in Vienna. At a bus stop they saw a woman, a little older than me, also without a swastika. They asked her the same questions they had asked me. Suddenly, they turned to me and dismissed me. I am grateful they did. Why, I'll never know. Nor will I ever know why they took me in the first place, nor what happened to the other woman who had to go with them. Where was she taken? Did she ever return?

I had other encounters. One day, soon after the Nazis had picked me up, I heard heavy boots following me. I crossed the street. The boots crossed the street. I crossed back. The boots crossed back. I walked faster, the boots sped up. I slowed down, there were those boots. I was petrified. Suddenly they caught up with me and a handsome young German soldier asked me politely if he could accompany me. What a relief! This was all he wanted—no camp, no atrocities—just company. I smiled at him. "I would be delighted if you do not mind accompanying a Jewish girl," I answered him. He clicked his heels, saluted, apologized, turned on his heels and disappeared.

One day when my mother was walking on the street, two SS men stopped her and ordered her to be at the main Market Hall at a certain time with a bucket and scrubbing brushes. My mother was naturally very scared and upset, and so was I. I felt I should substitute for her, but what would happen to her if I did? I felt awful, but I let her go and awaited her return in panic. She soon returned with our maid. Mary had gone there and made a scene: she proclaimed that she was a member of the Nazi party from way back; that my mother's three brothers had been officers in World War I, had been war heroes and that one had been killed on the Russian front; that my father had also been an officer during that war, had been badly wounded and decorated in the field; that my mother herself had worked for the Red Cross; and that my grandfather had converted his brewery into a field hospital (all facts perfectly true). Then she insisted that they let her employer go. They actually let mother go.

My mother was released and relieved. So was I, but my conscience has plagued me ever since. One should not be put to the test. My mother did not feel I should have gone instead of her, but I did. Mary was rewarded with most of our furniture when we left. She really saved my mother.

Our porter died the night the Nazis came to power and her son and daughter took over the management of the building. The son was now in an SS uniform but he behaved very correctly toward us. The two young boys who lived on the floor above us since our childhood also appeared in Nazi uniforms, but had forgotten that we existed. There were no more greetings or hellos on the stairs.

After the war, I visited the building where we had lived. The young woman, the porter's daughter, was still working there. She begged me not to tell anyone that her brother had been a Nazi. I had no intention of doing so. He had been perfectly decent. (Not all porters behaved well to the Jews who lived in the buildings they looked after.) The two young men who had lived upstairs found their reward—both were killed on the Russian front.

I continued my photo training until we left Vienna, but did not attend the Graphical Institute any longer. One day, I met one of my former colleagues from the Institute, a shy boy who had never talked to me at school. Now he stopped me and we had a long conversation. I suppose that he wanted to show me that he was not one of "them."

Hedy immediately stopped attending school after the Nazi takeover. She had two more years to go before matriculation, but there was no point in going. Books were being burned and many of the best authors' books were committed to the flames. Some of our non-Jewish friends sent their books to us rather than have them burned. A time of very intense reading followed for Hedy and me. We read the forbidden authors: Thomas, Heinrich and Klaus Mann, Friedrich Torberg, Bertolt Brecht, etc.

The Viennese, as a whole, behaved very badly toward the Jews. They went on a rampage; broke into homes; carted off the belongings of their rightful owners; confiscated Jewish property; "arianized" Jewish businesses without giving the owners proper compensation; and arrested innocent people for no reason whatsoever. They made life a living hell for all of us. All this, of course, was sanctioned and encouraged, even ordered by the leadership.

A young girl, a relative of mine, was forced to scrub the undercarriage of a car, to the amusement of the assembled crowd. Finally, a German soldier came to her aid, dispersed the onlookers and helped her up.

Non-Jewish friends of ours, whom mother helped in their time of need, ignored us on the street. We lived in fear and panic. Everybody who could leave, did; but it was very hard to leave. The borders were closed and where was one to go?

To get to the United States you had to get on a quota, somebody had to give you an affidavit, or you had to have a lot of money. And then it took a long time to complete the paperwork. France and Switzerland did not want you. You could go to England as a domestic after long bureaucratic delays. It was difficult to go to Palestine. We were like mice in a mousetrap. You could not visualize that life could become ordinary, routine, pleasant ever again. And, for many, it did not. Almost half the Jews in Vienna got out between March 1938 and September 1939, before the outbreak of the war. But in the countries later occupied by the Nazi hordes, escape became harder and harder and later almost impossible.

The Nazis confiscated your property and your money. Businesses had to be transferred to them. *Reichsfluchtsteuer* (a tax for leaving the country) had to be paid. We were not able to pay since our property was in Czechoslovakia and the Czech government would not permit money to be transferred to what was now Germany. My sister and I could go to Czechoslovakia under the auspices of our uncles. We did not have to pay *Reichsfluchtsteuer* since we were under twenty-one years of age; but mother could not get out legally because the tax had to be paid for her. My uncles arranged for a Czech police official's passport to be altered so that mother would appear on it as his wife. Of course, mother had to pay for it and pay she did. She also had to destroy her Austrian passport so it would not be found and cause terrible consequences. I had advised her to do that and then regretted my advice. Maybe she could have left

Czechoslovakia later had she had that passport. Who knows how to act under those circumstances?

We slowly wound up our household. The Persian carpets were put into storage. (After the war, I found out that they were removed from storage two days after mother's departure from Vienna. We never found out what happened or who took them.) The grand piano was sold to the Italian ambassador with the player piano and its many rolls for a pittance. My sister Hedy and her swimming friends had used the player piano a lot. The real purpose was to strengthen their leg muscles by using the pedals.

Mother gave most of our furniture to Mary, our loyal maid. She married soon after our departure. Knickknacks went to a musician who had played quartets with my parents in happier years. The ironing woman got linens and kitchen furniture. Books, silver, china and crystal were stored at Uncle Ludwig's house. We thought it would be safe there since he was a Czech citizen. Nothing was returned after the war. His sons claimed that the Nazis stole some things and the communists the rest after the war. Who knows?

After the Nazis occupied Vienna in March 1938 it was imperative that we leave and find a haven somewhere else. But where? One day my mother met a young American newspaper man and invited him for dinner. I do not know what she expected he could do for us—marry one of us, get us visas, be a good connection to have, take us somewhere, do something for us, or help in some way?

Anyway, he came and turned out to be a dreadful bore. Conversation was limited. I thought that my English was good but probably it was not. When we were small, mother and Father always spoke English in front of us when we were not supposed to understand them, but it turned out that mother's English was not good enough for conversation with our new friend.

My sister Hedy probably spoke no better than I did then, but the food in our home was as excellent as Viennese food could be so we sat over dinner forever, talking little and eating much. My sister and I yawned but our guest stayed on. The maid excused herself discreetly and went to bed. Hedy could not stand it any longer and disappeared; but our guest stayed. Mother and I were polite and continued whatever conversation we had going. At one point, he asked for something to drink. I interpreted it that he wanted water and went to the kitchen to fetch it. Finally, about eleven o'clock he excused himself and I took him downstairs. Apartment buildings in Vienna had porters who would let people in and out until ten o'clock. After that time apartment owners had to do it themselves. I took our guest downstairs and opened the door with the keys that were kept in the kitchen. I had to go to the kitchen twice—to get the keys and return them.

At six o'clock in the morning the doorbell rang and rang. We panicked. The Nazis preferred to pick up their victims at that time of the morning. Our maid ventured into the hall and we heard her scream. Hedy ran out to see what happened and we heard her scream. So now I ran out and found myself ankle-deep in water. The whole apartment was filled with water. What a relief—only a flood, not the Nazis. We were safe.

No one had ill intentions against us. The porter and the people living below us rang the doorbell. The water had leaked through the ceiling and awakened them. My mother or an insurance company had to pay damages, of course.

To this day I do not know what happened. Perhaps I did not turn off the faucet properly after filling the glass of water for our guest. I was in the kitchen twice that night. Was a washer loose, or was I too sleepy to hear the water running? Or was it ordained that we should have a wet exit from Vienna?

The atmosphere in Vienna was awful in 1938. We felt so isolated and deserted. Friends and relatives tried to get away. Everybody was, of course, totally absorbed with their own terrible problems. We did not know who was going where. To this day, I still do not know what happened to many of our friends and acquaintances. Did they get out? Did they survive? Where did they end up? None was in Vienna after the war. (Some did return, however, for various reasons.) I thought Tasmania would be the place to go. It was the furthest place on earth. I did not get there, but some friends did.

People I knew went to Shanghai, West Africa, South Africa, Cuba, the U.S., the Dominican Republic, Panama, the Philippines, Argentina, Brazil, Uruguay, Bolivia, Australia, England, New Zealand, and Palestine. Those that did not go far enough were caught in Europe later. Many friends and relatives perished. Grandfather's older sisters and brother perished in Theresienstadt, as did many in my father's family. Some of mother's old aunts (from the Wolf family) went to Israel and the U.S. at a rather advanced age and had a hard time adjusting to an entirely different life. The Hungarian family was simply wiped out. We, the younger generation, had a better chance to survive. We eventually adjusted to the change and made new lives for ourselves in other lands, but, at the time, life was grim and the future unimaginable.

Two or three days before Hedy's and my departure for Czechoslovakia, I bumped into my father. He had been released by the Nazis by then. I met him on the street by chance. This time, I did not avoid him but confronted him and told him of all my grievances against him: his dreadful, selfish behavior against mother; the anguish and heartache he had caused her and us; his egotism and his bad behavior toward us, his children; and that when Hedy almost died of pneumonia he never called, only sent some cheap candy over and did not try to help with expenses for the day and night nurses, etc. He was so taken aback by my outburst that he was left speechless. To hear all that from his usually subdued daughter! On that note I left him at the Schottentor (a square in Vienna). He survived the Nazis and the war. Having been married to a non-Jew and having false papers may have helped. He took refuge on Lake Balaton in Hungary for a while.

Finding a place of refuge was hard but leaving Vienna was not made easy by the Nazis either. We needed an exit permit. In order to get one, we needed a valid passport. This we had. Then we had to stand in line for hours to prove that the water tax, the income tax, sewer tax, and this tax and that tax were paid. Hedy and I were minors and not employed. (At the photo studio mother had paid for my training.) Yet, we had to stand in line for days in endless queues while SA and SS men paraded around with guns in holsters watching the Jews who tried to emigrate.

Once we had the papers together we had to make an appointment with a Nazi lawyer, get his approval and pay a fee. The lawyer we saw was tall, thin and curt. He stamped and signed the exit permit. I do not remember his name but he could have been Adolf Eichmann.

On June 28, 1938, the apartment was empty. A truck was waiting downstairs with our luggage. I ran back to look once more at the home of my youth—the beautiful large apartment in the third district with the built-in closets in the hall and the white tile stoves, which had been so hard to heat and had not kept the apartment warm in winter. Even the double glass panes with pillows between them and heavy drapes in front of the windows could not keep out the draft. A comfortable temperature had been hard to achieve in winter and the corridors and bathrooms were always cold except on the hottest summer days. I wanted to drink the wonderful Vienna water one more time and ran back into the kitchen to taste it.

Hedy and I went off by truck, my first ride in a truck. We were to meet mother at the railroad station, but had to go through customs first. Actually, going through customs was very funny. A little Austrian official was assigned to go through our things. The first thing he saw, however, was Hedy's photo album of herself and her swim team—all real bathing beauties. He concentrated on the photos and never looked at the rest of our things.

Mother and a friend of ours saw us off. mother was to follow a few days later with the Czech police official on whose passport she appeared as his wife.

We shared the compartment with a couple, both wearing swastikas pinned to their clothing. They looked very severe and never cracked a smile. Hedy cried bitterly when we left. She cried all the way to the border. As soon as we crossed into Czechoslovakia our fellow travelers took off their swastikas and expressed shame and sorrow about everything that had happened since March 11th.

Uncle Kurt met us on the Czech side of the border and drove us to Uherske Hradiste, the town where my mother was born and where he and his family lived. On the way I told my Uncle that Czechoslovakia was surrounded on three sides by Nazi Germany and wondered if we should try and sell the family brewery and transfer money abroad before it was too late. He replied that if all Czech Jews did that, the country would be severely damaged. He was so patriotic. Later, he changed his mind.

But now we were on our way. Aunt Gretl and our cousins greeted us at their home with a delicious lunch. mother arrived in Czechoslovakia on the police official's passport on July 4, 1938. Mother, Hedy and I stayed in Uherske Hradiste for a few days and then moved to Zlin.

CZECH INTERLUDE

(June 1938 - March 1939)

For many years our lives were ruled by failed world policies, and by an ambitious, ruthless, power-hungry, vicious, cruel, mad dictator who brought war and destruction to millions upon millions of people. This was a man who had no concern for individuals and who only cared about increasing his world dominance.

We were just leaves in the wind, blown here and there, without the power to make reasonable decisions based on logical determinations. We could not act, only react. Such was our world between 1938 and 1945 and, for millions it was impossible to react. Fate was so much worse for so many.

We were now in Czechoslovakia, a modern, prosperous, enlightened, highly industrialized democracy. It was a country of fifteen million people, carved out of the former Austro-Hungarian Empire after World War I. It contained most of the industrialized areas of the former monarchy. For many years the brilliant Thomas Masaryk had been the country's president; now it was Eduard Benes, a talented, humane man.

Under the Austrian monarchy, the Czech-speaking minorities did not fair too well; but now the Czechs had their own minorities—three-and-a-half million German-speaking Czechs, one-and-a-half million Polish-speaking Czechs, and one million Hungarian-speaking Czechs.

Soon after the Germans marched into Austria, Hitler cast his greedy eyes on this peaceful, prosperous country. Unending agitations and ever-increasing demands resulted. The German-speaking minorities were inflamed and agitated, particularly in the Sudetenland, where most of the German-speaking minorities lived.

My uncles had been able to get permission for mother, Hedy and me to live in Zlin where the Bata shoe factories were located. Thomas Bata, in his youth, was a poor shoemaker, but, through skill and intelligence, he was able to build the biggest shoe factory in the world in Zlin. He had studied American assembly methods and introduced them in his factory. Our beer from the family brewery was sold in Zlin and the Bata establishments were our best customers. My uncles were well acquainted with the Batas and, through the Batas' influence with the local authorities, we received permission to live in Zlin. The Czechs did not give permission to live anywhere in the country, just in one particular town or village. However, we were not given permission to work or prepare for an occupation.

The Bata shoe factory was totally self-sufficient. The surrounding forests belonged to Bata and provided the wood for heels. The cattle herds provided the leather. Bata had his own trains, railroad lines, airstrip and airplanes. The factories were extremely modern for that period. The main office building was a high-rise structure with Bata's office in an elevator that moved up and down and sideways so that employees did not have to waste time when they wanted to see the boss in his office. The office came to see the employees.

The company had its own hospital, medical services and profit sharing plan. There were modern schools for the younger employees where they received a fine education and learned the "ins and outs" of making shoes.

Everybody had to start on the assembly line, even the chief executives. It was a very paternalistic society. The married employees lived in company-owned red brick houses. The unmarried executives, engineers, doctors, lawyers, etc., lived in a company-owned high-rise hotel, the "Spolecensky Dum" where mother, Hedy and I also resided. Hedy was seventeen then and I was twenty years old.

We occupied a small suite, which included a little kitchen, but we took all our meals in the hotel restaurant where, for the first time in my life, I got acquainted with American canned food. I became very partial to pineapple in tins.

We were surrounded by young, eligible bachelors and would have had a wonderful time, but there was the constant saber rattling from neighboring Nazi Germany. We knew we had to move on, that peace was only an illusion. Our friend Sissy in England worked hard to get immigration papers for me.

Once a week, we were allowed to use one of the brewery's chauffeur-driven cars to make excursions into the surrounding areas—to Brno, Luhacovice, Pistian, Buchlovice, and to visit mother's aunts and uncles. It was fun to drive through the Czech villages. The streets were not paved and ducks swam in rainwater puddles. In the evening the herds were driven home through the villages. On Sundays and feast days the villagers wore gorgeous hand-embroidered costumes.

I took French, English and Czech lessons during that period given by the same teacher who had an atrocious accent. I read a lot but we had very little to do in Zlin. It was the only lazy period in my life.

One of our friends had to go on a trip to Egypt and asked Hedy and me to type articles from newspapers while he was gone. My typing was bad then, and has not improved since, but I spent hours doing it. When he returned from Egypt I proudly showed him my typed pages. He had forgotten that he had given us typing work to do. He probably had wanted us to improve our typing skills and to keep us occupied.

I had a few marriage proposals while living in Zlin but I was not ready to make a commitment or to settle down. However, immigration may have been easier with a partner.

Life would have been very pleasant in Zlin but there was disorder in the German parts of Czechoslovakia and, of course, resentment by the Czechs. The strange thing was that the Jews were German speaking and few spoke correct Czech. They only spoke German at home. The intelligentsia spoke mostly German. The oldest German university was Karl's University in Prague, and we heard many critical, even anti-Semitic, remarks from Czechs. We were only refugees and could not speak Czech yet.

In the early summer of 1938, I visited relatives in Morava Ostrava, a big industrial town. They had a houseguest, a famous German refugee painter, whose face was partially destroyed by shrapnel in World War I. He wanted to paint me but my visitor's permit could not be extended. I had to return to Zlin and was never painted by a famous painter or any other painter for that matter.

In August 1938, the Germans held maneuvers involving 750,000 men near the Czech border. The Germans tried to provoke the Czech military into action. Hitler spoke in Nuremberg on September 12, 1938 and tried to call forth an international crisis. He demanded self-determination for the Sudeten Germans or else.

On September 15th, Neville Chamberlain, the British Prime Minister, went to see Hitler in Berchtesgaden. He, and later France's Daladier, advised the Czechs to concede to Hitler's demands. Hitler kept increasing his claims. On September 24, 1938 the Czechs mobilized. All Czech men of military age joined their units. Within a few hours Czechoslovakia was fully mobilized. The situation was very tense. War seemed imminent.

Mother, Hedy and I fled from Zlin, which would have been a major military target. We went to a small but very pretty spa, Luhacovice. In case of war, Luhacovice should have been a much safer place.

It was a warm, sunny Indian summer. We stayed in a small pension and made our first personal acquaintance with a small persistent mouse that kept nibbling on the salami we had in our room. At first, Hedy and I did not realize who or what made those strange noises and we were scared out of our wits.

Some of mother's aunts from Morava Ostrava joined us in Luhacovice with their families. It was the last time I would see mother's lively, bustling, witty, roly-poly aunts (of the Wolf family). I remember one day walking in a beautiful sun-bathed park. A woman and a man were sitting on a bench surrounded by manicured lawns and flower beds. Half an hour later, I walked by there again. The man lay on the ground—dead. Was it an omen of things to come?

On September 29th, the Munich Conference was held. Chamberlain had flown to Munich and returned to London with a document signed by Hitler. He was hailed to have achieved "peace in our time." The heads of the British, French and Italian governments betrayed the Czechs. Peace in our time was achieved by terrible sacrifices by the Czechs. They had to acquiesce. The western democracies had deserted Czechoslovakia. The French were bound by a treaty to come to Czechoslovakia's aid. Had they aided Czechoslovakia, the Russians, too, would have come to their aid, but the western powers were biding for time and did not fulfill their obligations. I believe that was one of the reasons why Czechoslovakia fell into the Russian sphere of influence after the war. They were let down by the western democracies when they most needed help.

This last bit of news greatly disappointed the Czech demobilized men and the depression among the population was great. Grown men walked around with tears in their eyes. They had been ready to fight the Germans. Historians now believe that the Czechs could have successfully defended their country. Would we have survived in Luhacovice if war had come?

Czechoslovakia had to cede huge territories to the Germans. Territories where 2,850,000 Sudeten Germans and 700,000 Czechs lived were now incorporated into Germany. The Czech equivalent of the Maginot line fell into German hands. On Hitler's urging, the Poles and Hungarians now wanted a piece of the pie. The Poles received some territories on the Czech northeastern border. Hungary acquired portions of Slovakia. The remaining portion of Slovakia received full autonomy. What remained of Czechoslovakia was now strongly influenced by Germany. Hitler made all these territorial gains without losing a single soldier. Czech President, Eduard Benes, went into exile.

Mother, Hedy and I returned to Zlin. On October 31, we received orders to leave Czechoslovakia. We had no place to go. Returning to Austria would have been like a death warrant. mother could not even do that. She did not have a passport. There was great depression and helplessness among us. We were desperate. My uncles, with Bata's help, were able to extend our permits and our stay in Zlin.

The Batas were very decent to their Jewish employees and sent them abroad to Bata factories in England, Canada, South American, and the U.S. Finally, in the beginning of March 1939, everything was ready for me to emigrate to England. The trunks were packed. Mother had complete new wardrobes prepared for Hedy and me. I left Zlin and the pleasant life we had there to become a domestic in England. This was the only way one could get a permit to go to England. I said farewell to Grandfather's sisters, their families and to Uncle Heinrich. I never saw them again. The poor dears all perished in Theresienstadt, the ancient fortification where the Germans banished Czech and other Jews. None of the older Brauns survived this terrible ordeal. My mother's sweet, kind aunts, their loved ones, and Uncle Heinrich all ended their lives in this dreadful place. I said farewell to: Uncle Ludwig who was very ill and died shortly after my departure to mother's brothers and their wives; and my mother (Mutti) whom I never saw again.

When the time came to move on to England, I had to fly. Traveling through Nazi Germany by train had its perils. I started from Zlin and took a train to Prague. My mother saw me off in Zlin. We had walked through the snow to the little station. My luggage had preceded me. mother and Hedy walked behind my boyfriend and me. (Hedy was not ready to leave yet. She still needed a permit to travel to England.) I was so engrossed in my farewells to him that I hardly thought of my farewells to mother. Maybe I knew deep down in my heart and did not want to acknowledge that it would be the last time ever I saw her.

The train took me to beautiful Prague, where I spent three nights in an elegant hotel—but had to sleep in a bathtub. I guess no bedroom was available. Fortunately, when one is young one can sleep anywhere. I called my mother once more before my departure to England and spoke with her for what turned out to be the last time.

A relative saw me off at the airport with a huge bouquet of flowers. It was not a direct flight to London. I had to change aircraft in Rotterdam. The flight to Rotterdam was long and very bumpy. In Rotterdam, I got off the plane and walked a short distance across the field to the waiting plane. The wind was fierce and a gust of wind blew all my roses across the field. We departed in a plane with mostly English passengers. The down drafts in the small plane were awful. Everybody on the plane was airsick and we all made use of the little cups provided for this purpose. The English, however, as sick as they were, were much more genteel about the use of the cups than we mid-European barbarians. The torturous flight from Rotterdam to London finally ended after three hours of tossing and churning.

Two days after I left Prague the Germans marched into Czechoslovakia. On March 10, 1939, the total annihilation of that brave country began. It really was what remained of Czechoslovakia after the Germans, the Hungarians and Poles had robbed the land of vital territories the previous year. The Germans now occupied the truncated country. Czechoslovakia simply ceased to exist. Bohemia and Moravia, provinces in Czechoslovakia, became German protectorates. German troops occupied them. Mother and all the other Jews trapped in what had been Czechoslovakia, were in mortal danger, although they were not aware of it then. The Germans would soon (within two years) transport them toward the "Final Solution."

After Hedy, mother's brothers and their families and I left Czechoslovakia, Mutti moved to Prague and, as long as it was possible for her to do so, she wrote about her life there and how sorry she was to have let us go to England. (After the war started, our correspondence went through friends in neutral countries.) Mutti lived in the same building as one of my best schoolmates, Gretl

Kaufer, a bright, beautiful, vivacious girl. She, too, was sent to Theresientstadt where she died of typhus at twenty-two years of age.

Mutti and three of her cousins were ordered for deportation toward the end of 1941. They had to assemble at the main railroad station in Prague. We received her last farewell letter in Leamington Spa, England. The letter arrived when we were sitting around the radio. Japan had attacked Pearl Harbor. It was December 7, 1941 when we received this dreadful information.

We learned later that Mutti was deported to a German ghetto in Lodz, Poland. She supposedly remarried a friend from her youth in the ghetto. Her husband was said to have been taken away from her. Toward the end of 1944 she was sent from the ghetto in Lodz to Auschwitz. It was the last transport from Lodz to Auschwitz. The last time gas was used there.

Where was God? Where was justice? Our poor Mutti was only 55 years old. She certainly deserved better than such a dreadful fate. She was a good, kind, thoughtful woman, educated and innocent. She could not have hurt a fly. She should have lived to enjoy old age, her children and grandchildren. She is on my mind always. Poor dear Mutti.

I tried to help her get out of Czechoslovakia before the war started. I corresponded with Lord Russell. In reply to my letter he wrote that he was sorry but he could not help Mutti. He had helped so many Austrian refugees already. Suddenly, I received another letter from him. He felt badly about the first one. He now promised he would employ her and help me get the necessary papers. By then it was too late. War started soon thereafter. Poor, Mutti, dear.

I know millions of others suffered the same fate, but it was *my* mother, my one and only good, kind mother, and I mourn her.

My Great Grandparents **JOSEPHINE** and **SALOMON BRAUN**

b. 1830 m. 1855

My Grandfather Josef Braun and his brothers & sisters

I **SISTER SOPHIE** 1853—1900	II **GRANDFATHER JOSEPH BRAUN** 1855—1929	III **SISTER ESTI**	IV **BROTHER IGNATZ**	V **BROTHER JANOS**	VI **SISTER EMMA**	VII **BROTHER HEINRICH**	VIII **BROTHER LUDWIG**
Died of Tuberculosis. Never married.	m. Flora Wolf	4 Children Esti, her 3 daughters, her son-in-law, and her grandaughter, perished at the hands of the Nazis. Her son and his family fled to Palestine.	3 Children Was Josef Braun's partner in the brewery. His son and family fled to England. Two of his daughters were sent to Poland with my mother and perished there.	Was a lawyer in Vienna. 2 sons went to Uraguay.	Was killed in Theresienstadt. Never married.	Died in Theresienstadt. Never married.	2 sons returned to Vienna after W.W. II. One was in a concentration camp and married. They have no children.

I **GRETE BRAUN (MY MOTHER)** 1889—1944 m. Dr. Emmerich Back 1884 — 1957	II **DR. FRITZ BRAUN** (Chemist and Brewer) m. His Cousin Louise	III **ERNST** 1892—1915	IV **KURT BRAUN** 1895—1976 Gretl 1898—1981
SEE BACK FAMILY TREE	1 Daughter Susi Family fled to Palestine in 1939. Susi died in Haifa of insulin overdose. Fritz died in Teheran, and Louise returned to Vienna around 1960.	Was killed in Russia in W.W. I.	Herta is a Doctor in Great Britain, and has 3 children. Herta's youngest son lives in the U.S., a son and daughter live in England. 3 grandchildren Dr. Ernst Braun Scientist, married to a painter, fled with his parents to Palestine. The family joined Herta in England after W.W. II. 2 daughters live in England.

IGNAZ and **HERMINE WOLF** (My Great Grandparents)

1841-1906 1845-1932

M. 1864

My Grandmother Flora Wolf-Braun and her brothers and sisters

I **SISTER ERNESTINE**	II **BROTHER LEOPOLD**	III **GRANDMOTHER FLORA**	IV **SISTER ADELE**	V **SISTER GISA**	VI **BROTHER SANDOR**	VII **SISTER FRIDA**	VIII **SISTER ALICE**	IX **SISTER HELEN**
4 Daughters 3 fled to the US. 1 daughter Rosa, Rosa's daughter, Rosa's husband and her grandson, all perished at the hands of the Nazi's, in Budapest. Rosa's son Peter emigrated to Palestine.	**5 Children** Some fled to South America after the Nazi takeover. I have a lot of family in Argentina and Brazil. One son died in a motorcycle accident in Hungary in 1938. His daughter now lives in Vienna. Other Leopold Wolf decendents fled to Hungary. One of his grandsons perished in Hungary, at the hands of the Nazis.	1868—1920 M. Joseph Braun 1855—1929 SEE BRAUN FAMILY TREE	**5 Children** 4 fled to Palestine with their families. 1 son and his family fled to England.	M. Prof. Gomperz **3 Children** Oldest son emigrated to the US with family. Their daughter Lucie Rie emigrated to England and became famous as a potter. Younger son Paul was killed in WWI.	Founder of Sandor Wolf Museum He fled to Palestine after Nazi take-over and helped most of his relatives to join him there. He never married.	Fled to Palestine. No decendents.	Died in a coach accident. No decendents.	Fled with family to Palestine. Her decendents still live there. She had 3 children.

HERMINE and **LEOPOLD BACK** (My Father's Parents)

I **ELSE**	II **OSCAR**	III **MY FATHER** **DR. EMMERICH BACK**	IV **HILDA**	V **RICHARD**	VI **ALFRED**	VII **YELLA**
M. Oscar Fasal (an engineer) **2 Children** Daughter Gretl and husband were killed in Theresienstadt. Son Hans fled to the US. Married, but had no children.	(Musician) Daughter and son lived in Belgium. Daughter had 4 children and son had 2 children. All their decendents live in Belgium.	M. Grete Braun in 1917 divorced in 1936. Mother was killed in Auschwitz in 1944. Father's daughter and son from other marriages live in Vienna.	(Pianist) Married but had no children. Her husband was killed in W.W.I. She died of a broken heart.	(Lawyer in Berlin) He and his daughter, Hilde, fled to the US. Hilde's daughters live in the US.	(Lawyer) His only daughter disappeared in England after the beginning of W.W. II.	Emigrated to Holland Married, but had no children.

LORE LISBETH BACK (ME)
M. Jerry Waller in 1950

TOM WALLER b. 1951

LESLIE WALLER b. 1952
M. John Raftery in 1976
Christopher b. 1981
Lauren b. 1984

FAMILY LIVES IN THE US

HEDY BACK (MY SISTER)
M. Vasek Zahalka in 1943

JEANNY
Married and divorced:
Ken Kable

Son David

ANNE ZAHALKA
(famous photographer)

FAMILY LIVES IN SYDNEY, AUSTRAILIA

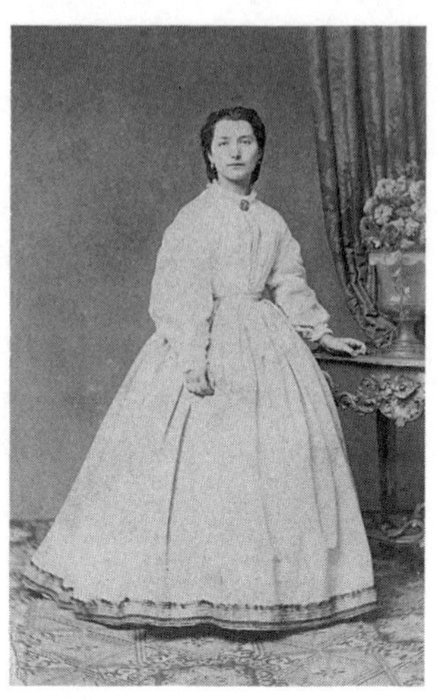

My great-grandmother Hermine Wolf
in 1863, at age 18.

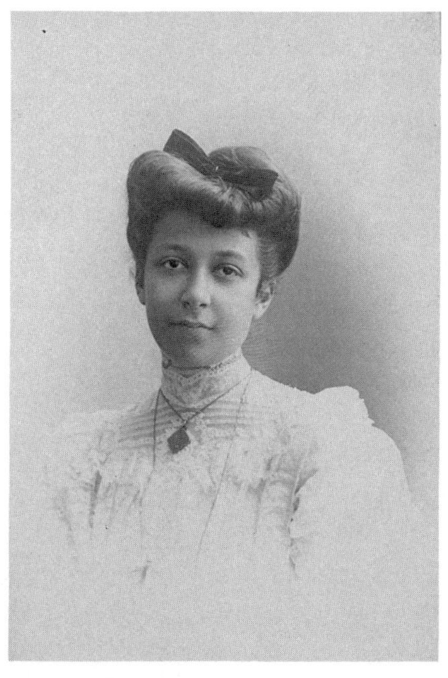

My mother ("Mutti") Grete Braun
as a young girl.

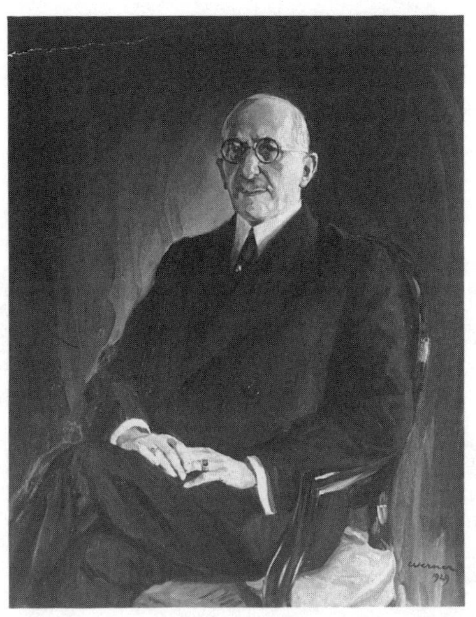

My grandfather Joseph Braun in 1929, at age 74.

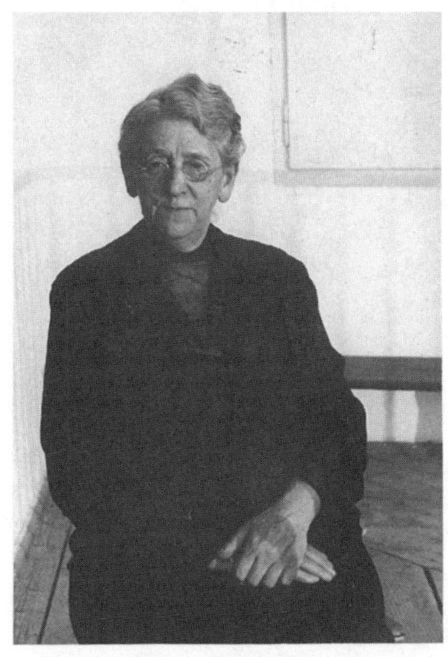

My grandfather Joseph Braun's sister, Esti Braun-Ehrenzweig, in 1932. She later perished in Theresienstadt.

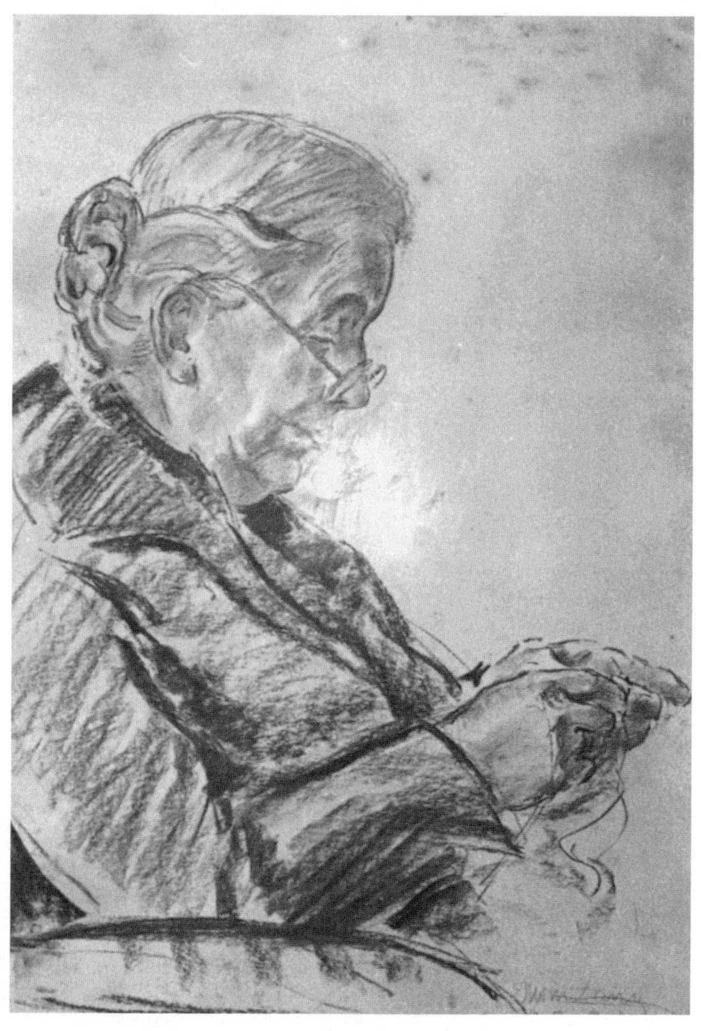

My great-grandmother Hermine Wolf in 1931, at age 86.

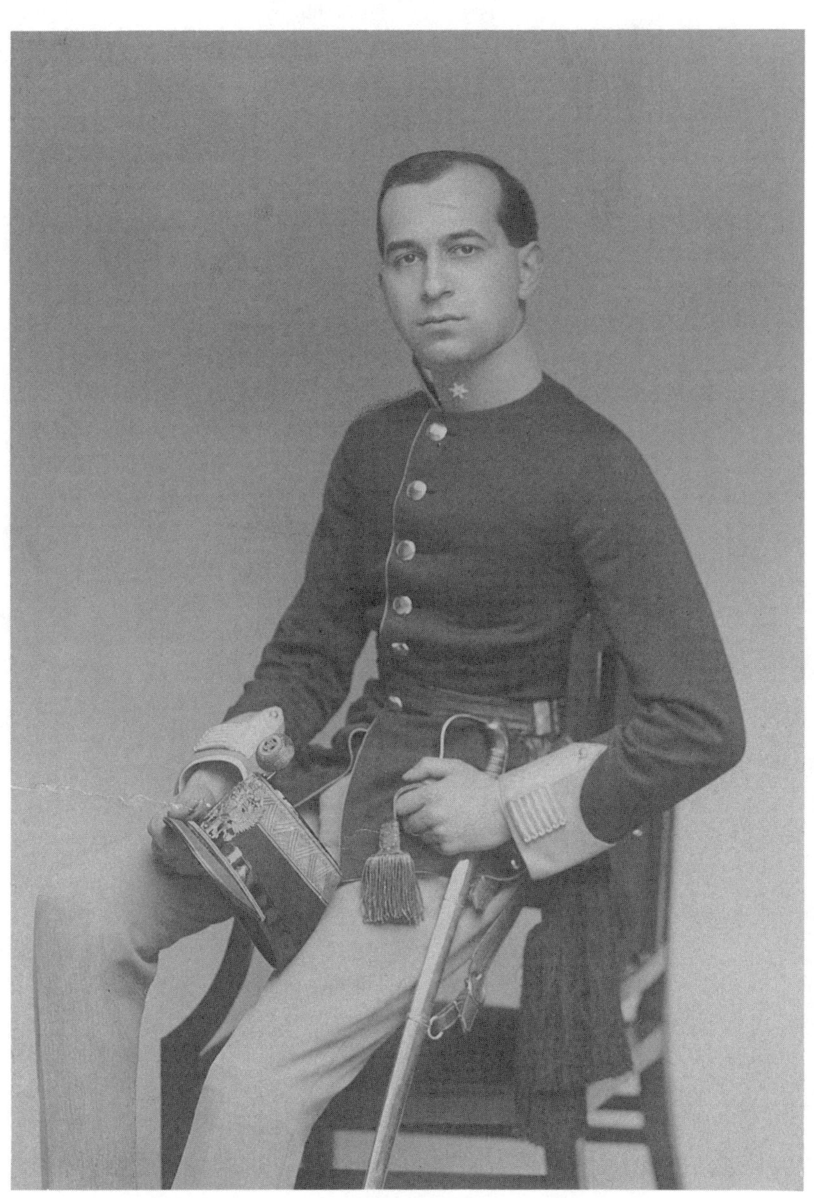

My father Dr. Emmerich Back during World War I.

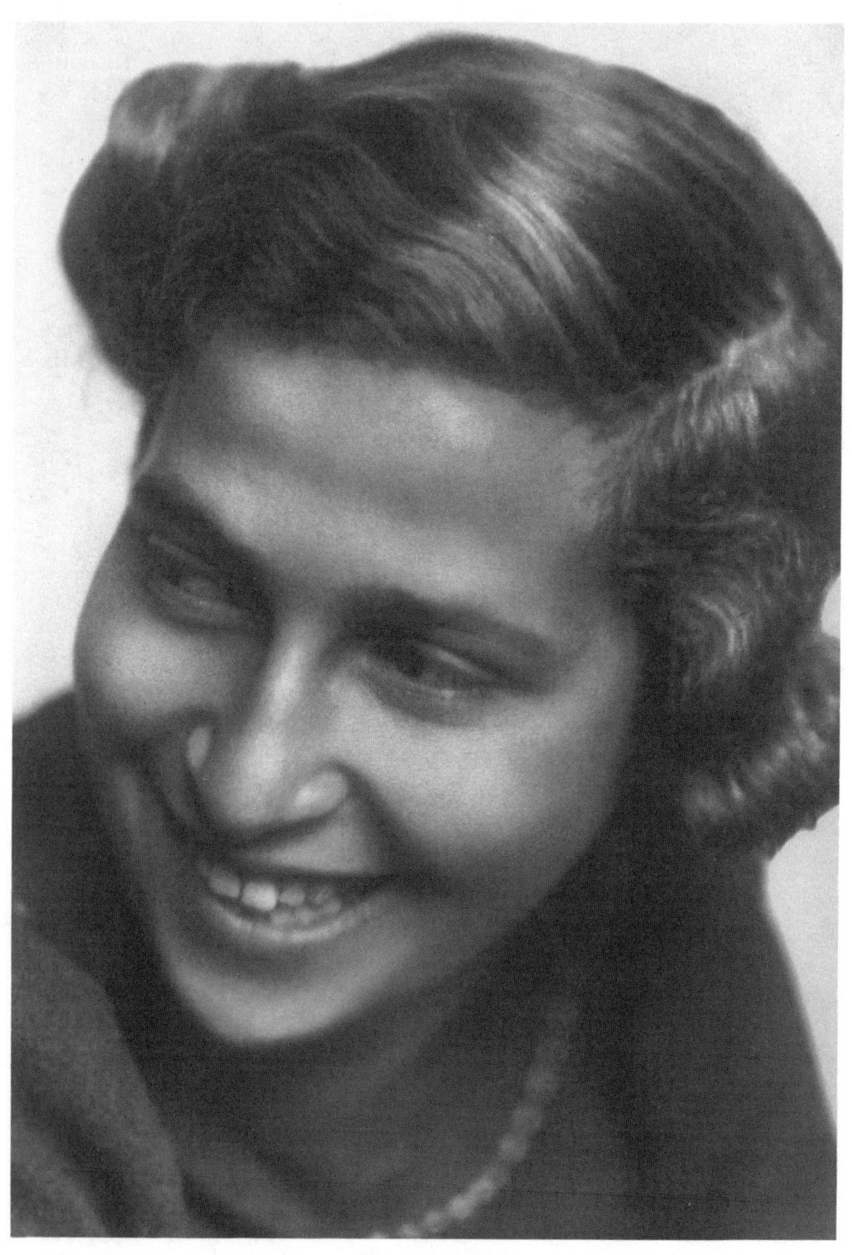

My sister Hedy in October 1937. (Photo by author)

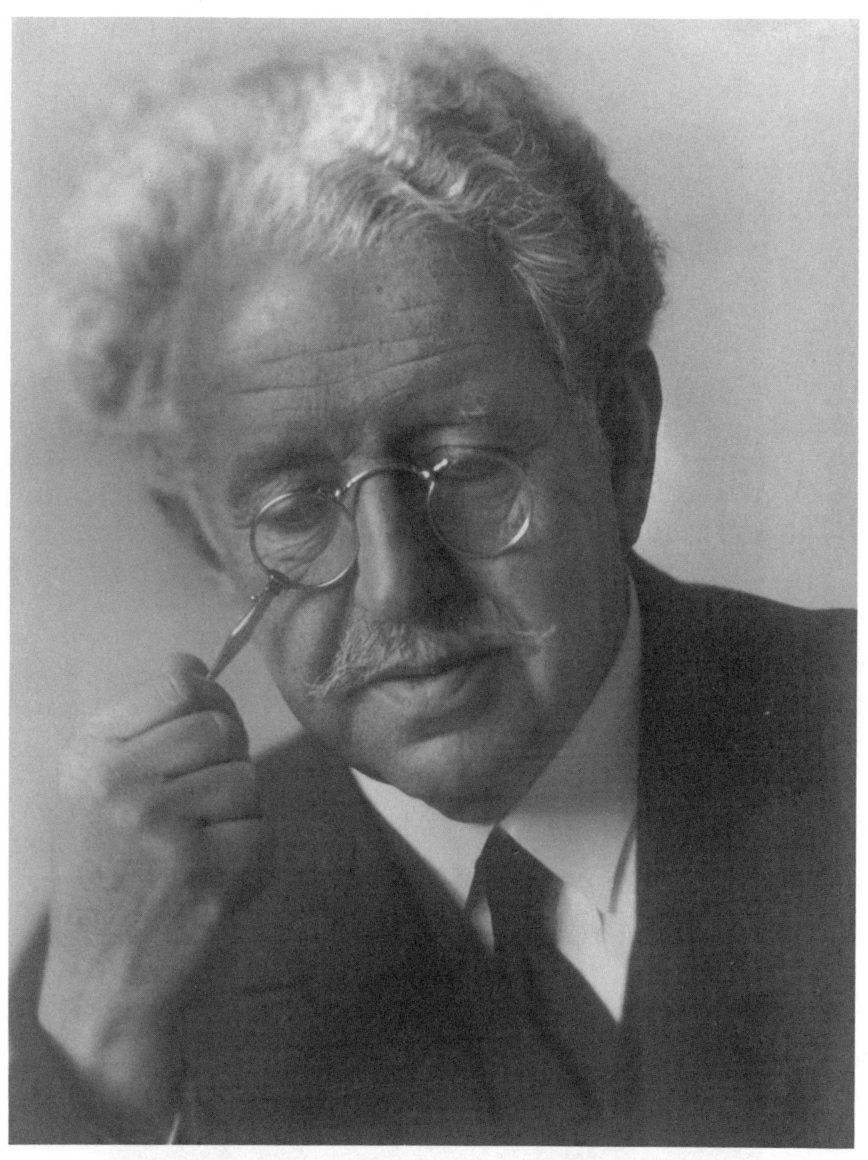

My grandmother Flora Wolf's brother, Sandor Wolf, in 1937. Sandor founded the Sandor Wolf Museum which was a wing in the Wolf family house in Eisenstadt. (Photo by author)

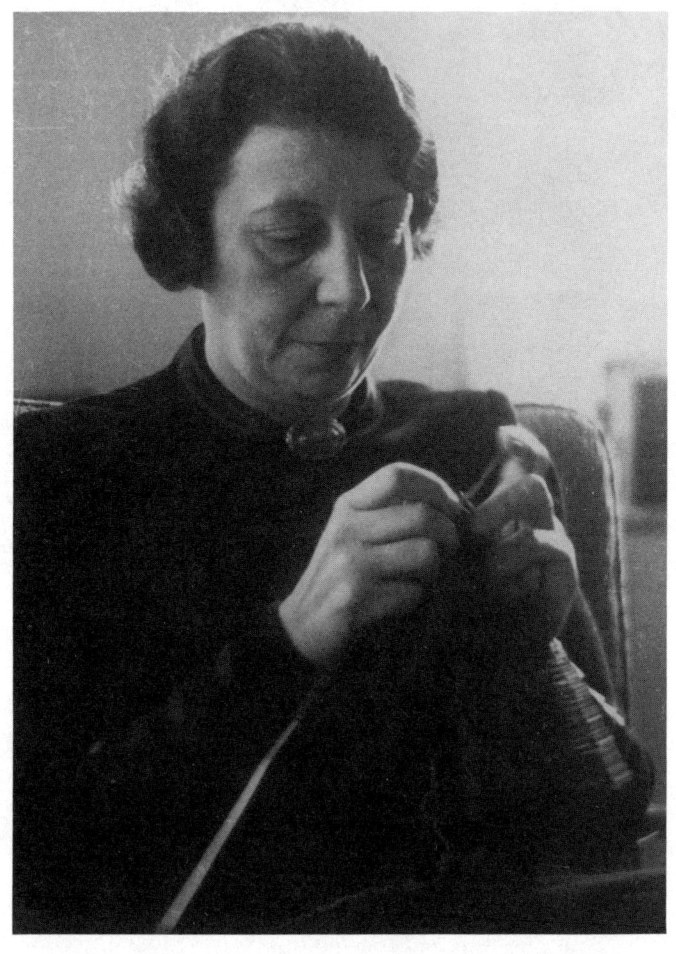

Mutti just before I left Czechoslovakia in 1939.
(Photo by author)

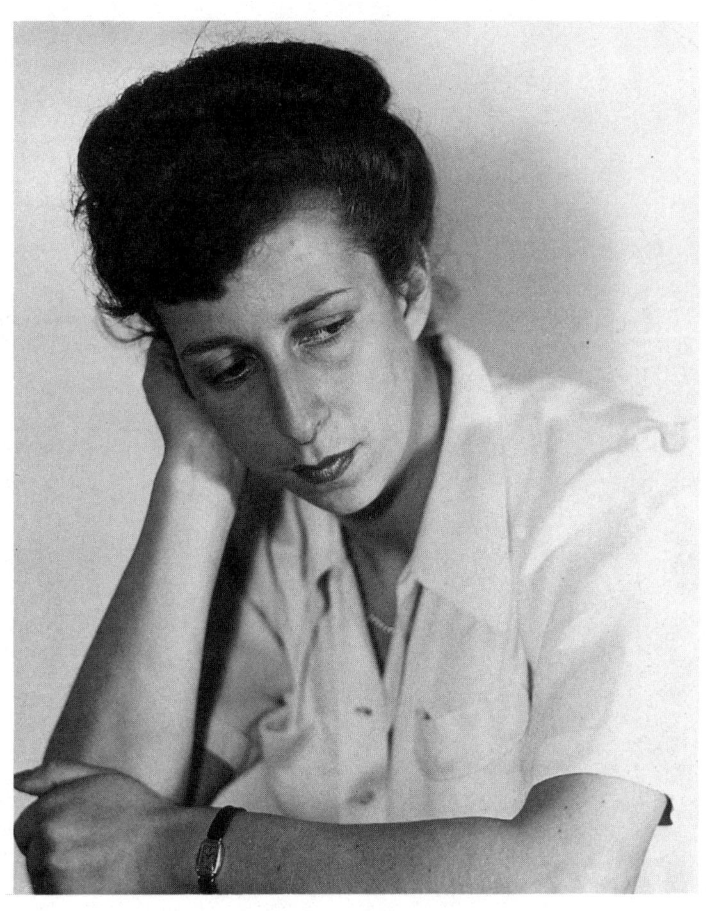

Me in Darmstadt, Germany in 1947 or 1948.

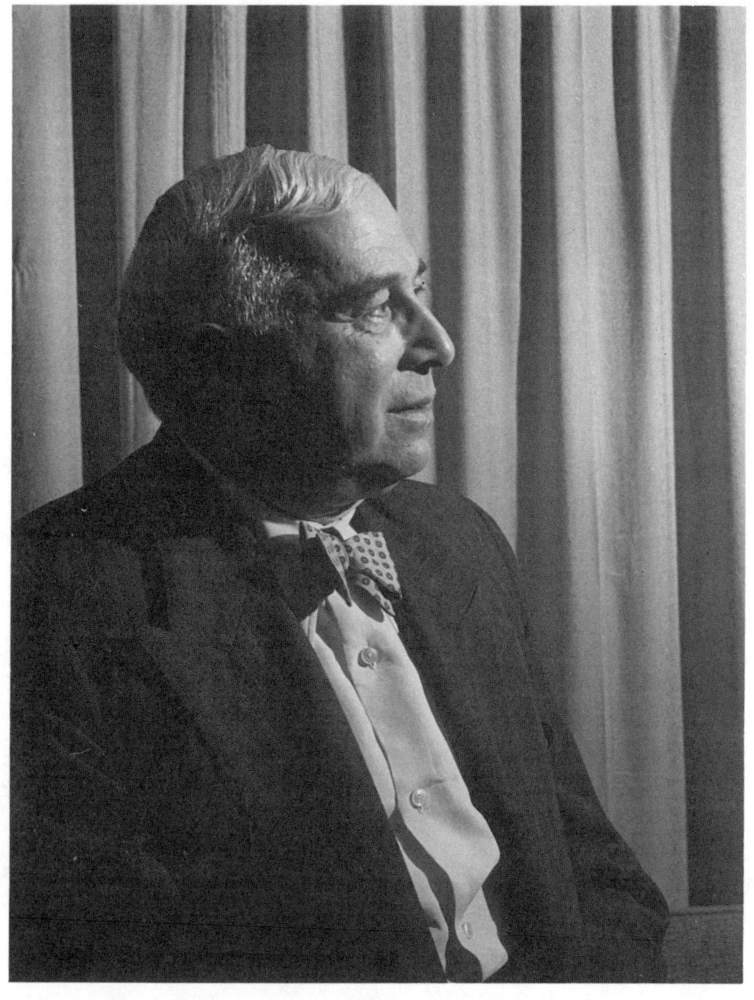

My father in 1952, at age 68. (Photo by author)

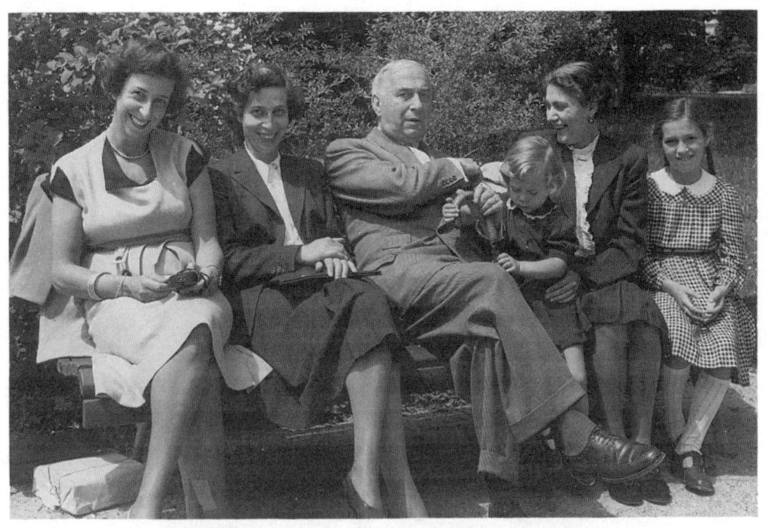

Family gathering in Bavaria in 1950, just before Hedy left for Australia. From left to right: me, Hedy, my father, Jeanny, Christa and Monica.

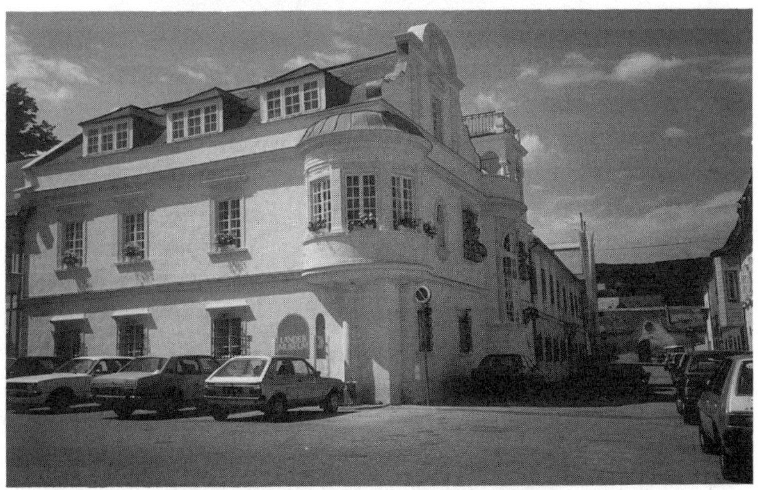

The Wolf family house in Eisenstadt. The left wing was Uncle Sandor Wolf's Museum. Today, all the connected structures are part of a museum. (Photo by author)

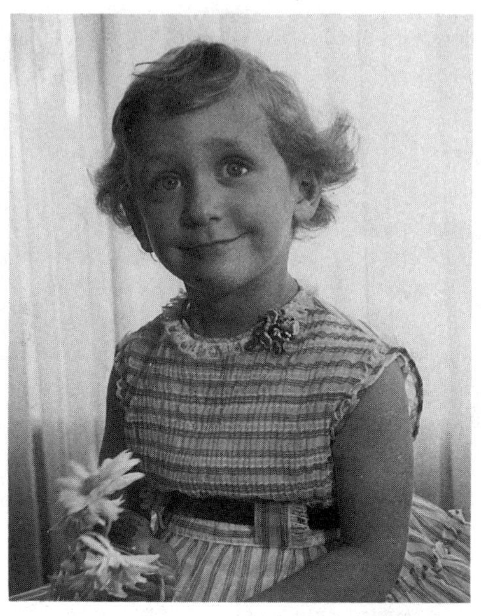

My daughter, Leslie Waller, now Leslie Raftery, in Los Angeles in 1955. (Photo by author)

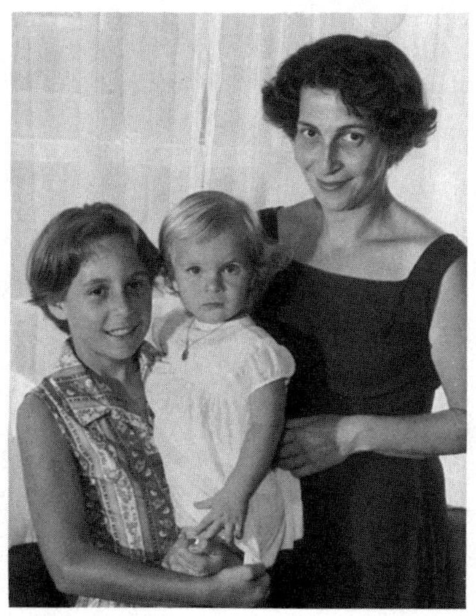

My sister Hedy in Australia, with her two daughters, Jeanny and Anne.

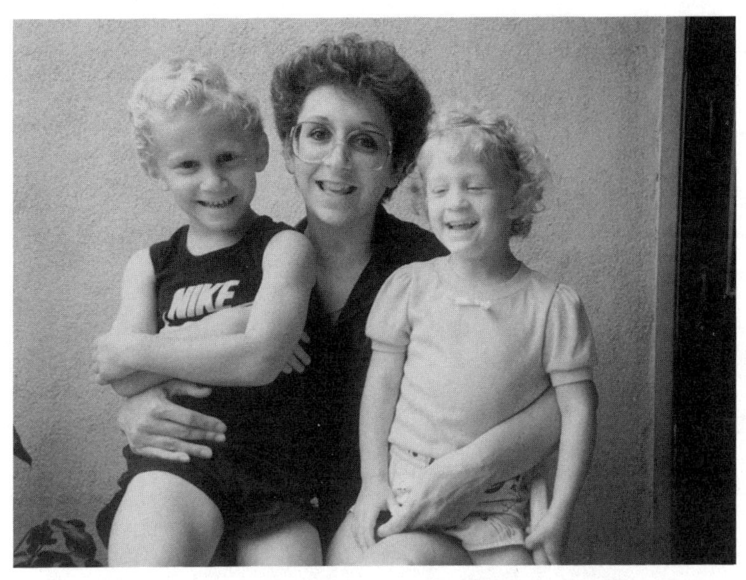

Christopher Raftery, my grandson, my daughter Leslie, and Lauren Raftery, my granddaughter, in Los Angeles in 1987. (Photo by author)

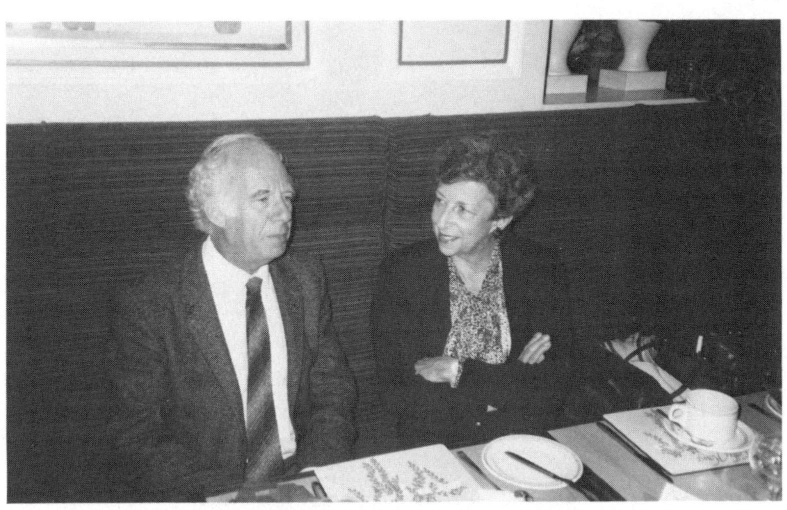

My cousin, Professor Ernst Braun, and me in London in 1988.

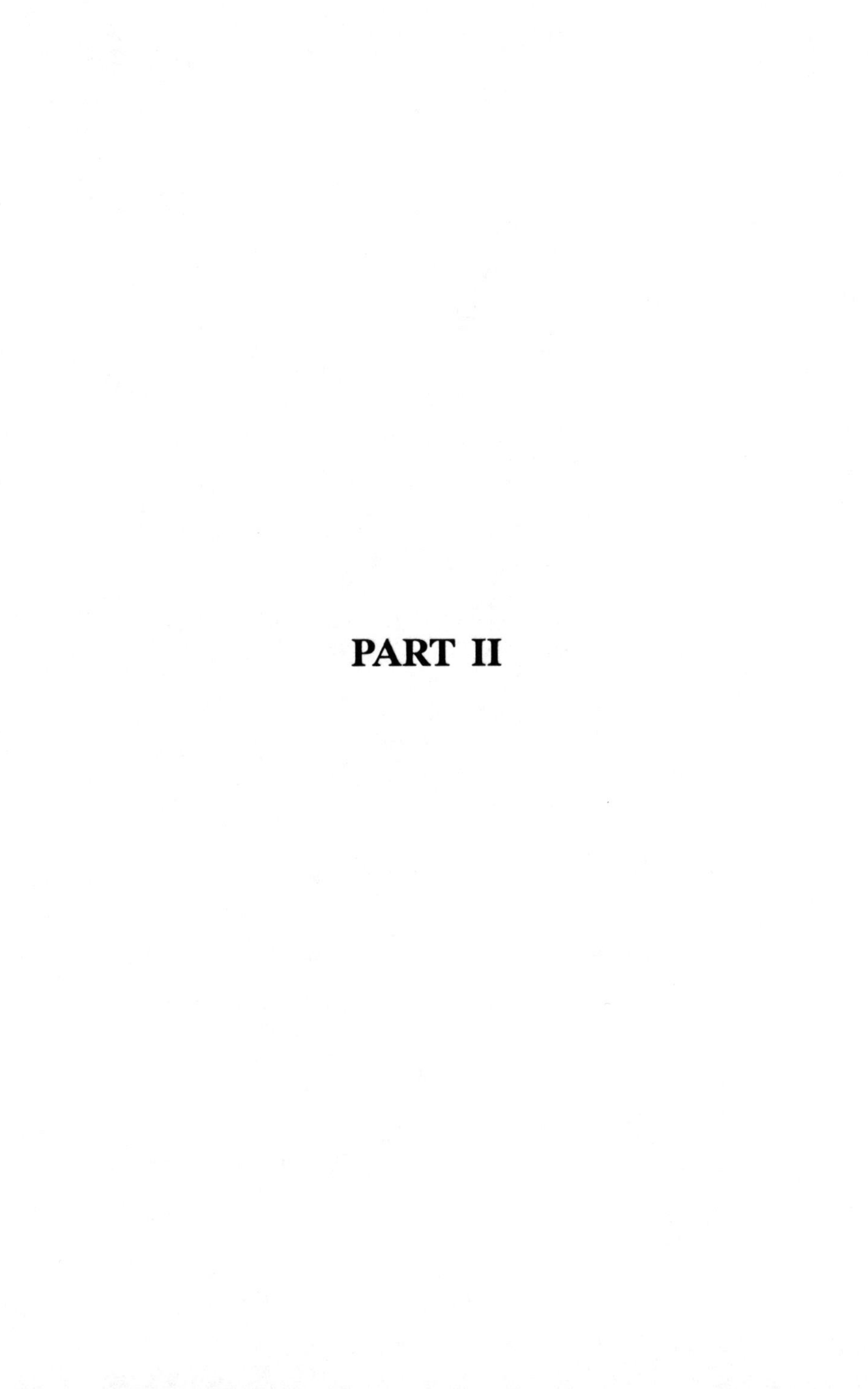

PART II

ARRIVAL IN ENGLAND

I left my mother, family, friends, my childhood, the language of my youth, comfortable circumstances, and the familiar landscape behind and ventured forth into the unknown alone. I was twenty-one years old, spoiled, inexperienced and almost penniless.

On March 8, 1939, more than fifty years ago, I flew for the first time in my life. My generation was the first to be able to visit far off places, see the vast oceans, the high mountains, the deserts, and distant islands; see the polar regions from above; be in and above the clouds; follow a sunset or a sunrise; meet people from different cultures and civilizations; return to the continents from whence we came; and learn about each other, and understand different lifestyles. We also had the newfound opportunity to become better acquainted with the world we lived in—the history of its people, their art, their music, their architecture, the food they eat, their habits, their languages. Flying is safe, fast, clean and convenient. Flying has always been a wonderful adventure for me and a window seat indispensable, although not always available.

The employer Sissy, my mother's tennis partner, had found for me was at the airport. Mrs. Carr was an extremely pretty, lively woman. Lucie Rie, my now very famous cousin, or rather mother's youngest cousin, was with her. Lucie Rie was then a struggling potter but now is recognized as the world's foremost potter. The Queen awarded her the CBE[11] and the OBE[12], two very prestigious honors. (Recently she became Dame Lucie Rie.) I had to promise Mrs. Carr that I would stay with her for at least six months. She promised to pay me five shillings per week as her au pair.

Mrs. Carr drove me in her small Morris Minor to Old Windsor. There I met Anthony and David, my two little charges, and Mr. Carr. A few minutes after our arrival, dinner was on the table—no lengthy cooking procedure like in Vienna. The meat was awful. I was convinced I was eating dog meat. I soon found out it was mutton. I had never eaten lamb before and I still do not like it.

The next morning, I realized that the Carr's little bungalow was situated along the Thames River. The landscape was lovely. There were weeping willows along the towpath[13] and punts[14] and little schooners on the river. The whole landscape was shrouded in a slight mist that added to its beauty. The house was small and messy, everything was very informal.

A few days after my arrival, the Nazis took over what was left of Czechoslovakia and now it was impossible to have money sent to me. (mother had intended to do so on a monthly basis.) My au pair status was quickly changed to mother's helper and Mrs. Carr paid me ten shillings per week. She soon went to work, maybe to

---

[11] Commander of the British Empire.

[12] Order of the British Empire.

[13] Before boats were motorized, a path by the side of a river was used by horses to pull boats.

[14] Punts were narrow, shallow boats propelled by poles.

earn money to pay me the extra wages. In any case, I had to do all the housework, some of the laundry, the cooking, and take care of the children—something the average housewife does, but I had not the slightest idea how to do it.

Everything took me a long time. I tried to clean the room that the little boys and I shared so thoroughly that hardly any time was left to do the rest of the house. I will admit that I was a very poor domestic, and, on top of that, I had a poor attitude. All my Viennese domestic friends earned the traditional one pound per week. At ten shillings, I felt exploited.

Distant relatives of mine had taken refuge in London. I went to see them on my days off. They were wonderful to me and I looked forward to seeing them. Before food was rationed, they prepared some of my favorite dishes and I had a wonderful, warm place to visit.

I had been lucky—I got out of Vienna and Czechoslovakia just in time. I was able to arrange a place where Hedy could work as a domestic. A very dear friend of ours, Doctor Rosenfeld, was very active in helping members of Hedy's swim club to emigrate. He helped innumerable people get to England and he helped Hedy, too. She followed me in April. She had to travel through Nazi Germany by train. She was young enough to go on a children's transport. She often talked about the heart-rendering scenes she witnessed as the train progressed through Germany. Jewish parents were saying farewell to their children; they were sending them to the safety of England. The poor parents had to stay behind in Germany and face the terrible fate that followed.

I was in England now, but mother, my uncles and their families were still in Czechoslovakia. My uncles tried to sell the brewery and two German brothers, who were brewers, bought it. They even paid a decent amount for it, but the occupying Nazis confiscated the money. After the war and endless struggles with German restitution offices, we got a tiny amount as compensation. Uncle Kurt, Aunt Gretl and their son, Ernst, went to Palestine where they spent the war years. I managed to get their daughter, Herta, then sixteen, to England as a student nurse in the London Hospital. She eventually studied medicine and is now a public health doctor in South Wales. Aunt Gretl's father hanged himself. He did not feel he was young enough to withstand the changes required to settle in Palestine. However, Uncle Fritz and his family did go to Palestine.

Mutti was left behind in Czechoslovakia. When she left Austria posing as the wife of the police official, she had destroyed her passport. Someone may have been able to get her a false passport, but she was not anxious to leave. She did not see the danger she was in. When the Nazis occupied Vienna they came with a vengeance. In Prague they did not use such excesses—they had other plans: the complete extermination of the Jews.

CULTURE SHOCK

I was never ready or prepared for the big changes that were to take place in my life and found them totally bewildering. I had studied English and English history and loved to read English literature. However, England, its people, its customs, its climate, its food were a total surprise to me.

I knew the English through Shakespeare, through Galsworthy's beautiful novels, but not as real live people. They were very different from the Austrians, much more reserved, more formal. For example, they did not always shake hands. At first, when they did not shake my hand I became very sad and thought they did not like me. The English also did not talk about intimate details of their lives as the Viennese did. They said, "How do you do?" but did not want to know how one did. Conversation was mostly about the weather—what a fine day it was, or wasn't. The weather was really something to talk about. They were always friendly to your face, but gossiped a lot behind people's backs.

I blundered terribly on my second or third day in England. When asked how I liked my roast beef, I answered that I liked bloody roast beef. The conversation, even the air, froze. I was avoided and I did not know why.

Going to bed at a time before electric blankets or central heating was awful. Bedclothes were so damp and bone-chilling, it took hours to get even somewhat comfortable in bed. When asleep, if even one toe would move, I would be chilled to the bone, again. The open fireplaces just warmed your front. You had to be so close to the open fire to get any warmth that you developed miserable chilblains.[15]

I loved London, especially big, beautiful Hyde Park with sheep and little lambs grazing on the lawn and herds being driven across busy Bayswater Road in the morning and at night. What a strange spectacle this was.

One day, walking through Hyde Park toward Kensington, I saw the oddest sight—lancers on horseback with pale blue medieval breastplates and helmets. One of the King's guard regiments was riding toward me. I thought I was dreaming. Then I saw men in knee-socks, short skirts and huge bearskin hats blowing on weird instruments and walking in measured steps.

I was totally confused seeing traffic on the wrong side of the street. On which side of the street would I get on the bus to get back to Old Windsor?

Why did I not know all this? Why was I so unsophisticated? So confused? An average tourist had this knowledge and now I was a resident of England and totally bewildered.

There were so many different do's and don'ts. I loved England, its people, its lovely little towns, its square Norman church towers, its soft, rolling landscape, the fragrant spring air, even the cold blustery winds, but it took me a long time to get used to all of it.

So much confused me in England: weights, measures and money (20 shillings to a pound, 21 shillings to the guinea, 12 pence to a shilling). Yet, I was fascinated by London and did a lot of sightseeing by myself or in the company of former Viennese or Czech friends. There was

---

[15] Chilblains are a skin inflammation caused by extreme temperatures (either hot or cold).

a group of Bata employees in London. I saw a lot of them in the beginning before the war started. One of the young men wanted to marry me. He had already proposed in Prague before I went to England. He was a very nice, serious young man and wanted to take me to America. But he was not glamorous enough for my taste and I could not make up my mind. So, it was "no." He cried at my response. He did not go to America but became a millionaire in England.

I had seen poverty before, but not slums. And London indeed had slums! In those areas, there was extreme poverty and unemployment. And, yet, the people who lived in these parts of town seemed cheerful and jolly and had a great sense of humor. It was very hard for me to understand them. When they spoke, they dropped the letter "h" in words where it was appropriate, and added an "h" where none existed. Thus, "has" became "as" and "is" became "his." I was confused enough already.

Social distinctions were made according to the use of the English language. In Austria, the aristocracy made a point of speaking in dialect, but in England you did not belong to the upper class unless you spoke the King's English. And I spoke in the accent of the enemy. In Austria and Czechoslovakia I had been very popular with young men. In England, young men were hard to meet. In the six years that I lived in England, I may have had two or three dates with young English men. During the war with Germany, I am sure it did not help to speak with a German accent. It did not make matters easier. Now, as a domestic, I was socially not an equal, and, to what I considered my equals, not acceptable.

I was not prepared for sex, either. I was twenty-one years old when I left Czechoslovakia and last saw my mother, but sex was never mentioned or talked about and no one took me aside to explain its mystery. I entered a strange, unknown world totally innocent and unprepared.

NOT QUITE WAR YET

Hedy arrived in England shortly after I did. Mrs. Carr and I picked her up at Victoria Station and took her to Old Windsor. We had to share a bed that first night. Hedy tried to occupy the whole bed and pummeled me all night long.

My cousin, Herta, arrived in England before Hedy and I had to give her half of the sixty pounds I was allowed to bring to England. I had thirty pounds left and now Hedy was to receive half of that. Soon my luggage arrived and I had to pay eight pounds for it leaving me with seven pounds, my nest egg. I did not touch those seven pounds through all my years in England—through the war, through hardships. This was set aside for emergencies and, when I left England, I had the seven pounds with me plus the interest it had accrued.

Mr. Carr went to the city every day. Mrs. Carr took him to the nearest railroad station in the morning and picked him up at night. I took the Carr children to nursery school every morning. We walked along the lovely river, crossed through an ancient little cemetery and passed a broken-down little Norman church with chipped tombstones and little rabbits popping in and out of the tombs and frolicking between the graves and willow trees. It was sheer beauty.

It was so lovely along the river. I walked often with the little boys toward the locks and watched the slow progress of the boats through them.

Being a domestic was really not my thing. I have never been good at nor interested in domestic duties, and looking back at this period of my life, I now come to the conclusion that Mrs. Carr was a very nice, efficient woman. She put up with my ineptitudes with equanimity.

We were very close to Windsor Castle and saw the royal family, the king, the queen and the two little princesses several times. Once, I saw them getting into the coach with the French foreign minister, Monsieur Bonnet. The Queen, now Queen mother Elizabeth, was much better looking than her photographs suggested. Her coloring was beautiful—dark hair, violet eyes and a translucent skin.

On Easter Sunday, we observed the whole royal family from Windsor Great Park. A band was playing below a terrace and they were all assembled to listen. Princess Margaret was quite mischievous. She had gotten hold of a pulley and pulled a blind up and down until she was told to cease and desist. But it was funny for the onlookers to see all the royalty disappear and reappear at the pull of a cord.

Mrs. Carr was very good at rowing and punting (using a pole to propel a boat) and she participated in regattas. We all went to watch her win prizes. One day, she took me to a big celebration at Eaton College. There were fireworks and society ladies on the beautiful ancient college grounds. Another time she took me to a celebration on Runnymede Island, an island on the Thames not far from Old Windsor where the Magna Carta had been signed by King John in 1215. Tents had been put up on the lawn. The trees and vegetation were lovely and the evening was balmy. All this was very new to me but it enabled me to enjoy a taste of prewar England and the last summer of peace.

The Carrs had German friends who had a bungalow alongside the tributary to the Thames. It was across from Windsor Great Park. I made friends there with a young German, Heinz. Of course, I told him that I was Jewish, but he still came to see me by boat. We went punting and talked about how in Germany we could not have been in the same boat together. When war approached and he had to return to Germany, Heinz's farewell was very emotional. Whatever became of him?

During the summer of 1939, Mrs. Carr had two French teenagers at the house. They were a lot of fun and very noisy. We all had to eat the awful fish they had angled out of the Thames.

The political situation became worse every day. Hitler now wanted the Polish Corridor and Danzig. He tried to inflame the German-speaking population of Danzig as he had done before with the Austrians and the Sudeten Germans. On August 23, 1939, the Germans signed a pact with the Russians and war was now imminent. Hitler wanted "his" war; there was no holding him back.

I went to see "All Quiet on the Western Front" with the two French boys. They were in tears over the film and the prospect of returning to France and the war. They, too, bid emotional farewells, as did the young Swiss girl who I had befriended during the summer. She was the vicar's au pair. They all had to return home to a very uncertain future.

WAR

On Friday, September 1, 1939, I was scrubbing the floor of Mrs. Carr's living room when she turned on the radio. It was announced that at 4:30 a.m. on September 1, 1939, Nazi troops had started pouring into Poland. There was no turning back; it was war. Hitler used terrible lies as justification for his deceit and aggression.

After World War I, through the Treaty of Versailles, the Poles were awarded an outlet to the sea, the Polish Corridor. There had been a lot of agitation among the German-speaking population. Germany now wanted this territory and the free city of Danzig. This became the reason for Hitler's invasion. Prime Minister Chamberlain informed Germany on September 1 that Britain would go to war unless the German troops were withdrawn from Poland. That was, of course, the last thing Hitler intended to do.

The House of Commons met Sunday, September 3, and Chamberlain informed them that a state of war now existed between Germany and Great Britain. France also joined that day in a declaration of war.

I was polishing Mrs. Carr's living room floor when the Prime Minister made this declaration of war. Here it was—Hitler had his war. We were all dragged into this, all Europe, all the world. Six years of war followed and millions of casualties and victims.

Gas masks were distributed; houses were blacked out; and there were no street lights. The few cars that were able to obtain gasoline had to drive without lights. We navigated through the dark streets with flashlights and were often admonished to turn them off. Rationing of food and clothing followed shortly.

On the second or third day after war was declared there was an air raid alert. I was home with Mr. Carr and the little boys. On his advice, we all sat under the dining room table waiting for the bombs to fall, but nothing happened. We felt very sheepish when the "all clear" sounded and crawled out from under the table. Mr. Carr continued to go to the city every day and Mrs. Carr started to work for the Red Cross.

Poland with its cavalry regiments was unable to withstand the onslaught of the German panzers and airplanes. Poland was annihilated very quickly. Soon Germany's new ally, the Soviet Union, took part in the spoils. Their invasion of Poland started on September 17. On September 29, the Germans and Russians divided up Poland.

The German conquests in the East made the final solution, the destruction of the Jews, possible for Hitler. This was a policy he followed to the very end of his life.

In England, meanwhile, nothing much happened until the invasion of France and the Low Countries (Holland, Belgium and Luxembourg) and the great air attacks that started in the fall of 1940. For seven months we lived through the "phony war." This period gave us a chance to prepare for the real thing.[16]

Soon after the outbreak of war our "refugee status" changed to "enemy aliens." There were curfew and travel restrictions imposed on all the refugees from territories now dominated by Hitler. But all this was made easier by the politeness and pleasantness of the British officials.

---

[16] The "phony war" was the period of time between the fall of Poland in September 1939 and the German attack on Denmark and Norway in April 1940.

1939 - 1940

I had promised Mrs. Carr that I would stay with her until September 1939, but I stayed on until Christmas. After New Year's, a Czech friend of mine persuaded me to leave Mrs. Carr and move in with her and her husband. They had a nice flat in Chelsea and she expected a baby shortly. I felt that Mrs. Carr did not pay me enough, but Eva paid me even less—nothing!

I needed income and soon found a job in the country. The house was quite a distance from the railroad station. One evening in February 1940, I was coming back from London in the blackout. I got off the train, not realizing that the train would be brought into the station in two segments. When I got out, there was no station and I found myself rolling down an embankment that was much lower. I rolled all the way down. My foot hurt terribly, but I managed to walk to the house.

In the morning when my alarm clock went off, I was to bring an early morning pot of tea to the family. I turned to get up and suddenly I was in agony. The bone, which apparently broke the night before, must have shifted. This was the first of many, many broken bones I have suffered throughout my life. I could not walk. When the family did not look, I crawled. I had no money and no insurance. I did not know where to go or what to do. I called our former family doctor and he told me to come and see him. Equipped with a stick and a slipper I limped to him through the blackout in a strange area. I could not find my way and asked people for directions.

I was sent here and there. I was crying in frustration and pain, but finally I got to him. He was no longer a doctor, but a butler. At least he was able to tell me where to go and what to do.

My best friend, Liesl, was in London, married and very pregnant. She came with me to the hospital. In the hospital they first wanted to take care of her, but finally my foot was X-rayed, set, and put in a cast. I stayed with Liesl's parents until I could shed my cast.

I eventually found another domestic job with a wealthy German refugee family, the Koerners, in Bath. Hedy, too, was in Bath at that time. I looked after two little boys and a grandmother. Mrs. Koerner was in London and I was alone with my charges. They did have help in the house, though. I wore a nanny's uniform and took the children, David and Tony, to the magnificent park across from "The Crescent" an area with beautiful Georgian homes. I have a vivid memory of my time in Bath—the hilly streets and the heavy baby carriage I had to push uphill with little Tony running ahead of me. He would not stop when I called him; I was deathly afraid I would lose him.

When Mrs. Koerner was in Bath she entertained often. The famous Austrian author, Stefan Zweig, was a frequent visitor. He was a very charming man and spoke in a very distinct Austrian dialect. One day he brought me a little bunch of flowers. I was terribly thrilled. When foreigners had to hand in their photo equipment I asked Stefan Zweig, who was by then a British subject, to keep it for me. He gave me a receipt, which I still treasure. The poor man soon moved to Brazil and committed suicide with his wife. His "World of Yesterday" had vanished and he could not bear to live in the ugly new world.

On May 10, 1940, during the time I lived in Bath, Hitler invaded France, Belgium and Holland.

We had to leave Bath as soon as the British admiralty moved there. "Enemy aliens" could no longer reside there. We moved to London and to the Koerners' elegant apartment at Princess Gate, an elegant square in London. I took the children in little silk outfits to Kensington Gardens. I wore a starched uniform and met real nannies and their charges. I spent hours each day polishing the perambulator. The British authorities interned Mr. Koerner. He was held in some barracks in Kensington. I walked the children by the barracks every day at a given time so he could see them.

One day I walked near Marble Arch and bumped into Mrs. Carr. She was crying bitterly. I asked her why the tears. She had just come from the American Embassy in Grosvenor Square and had completed the arrangements to send her little sons to America for the duration of the war. Shortly after that, it was Mrs. Koerner's turn to arrange for her little boys to be evacuated to America.

London was no longer safe for little children and we busily prepared for their departure. The farewells were very sad. The Koerners did not see their children again until late in 1946. The children did not recognize their parents when they returned from California.

France had fallen. The British expeditionary force had to withdraw through Dunkirk. Somehow the British press had presented this as a big victory but, of course, it was not. At least 200,000 British soldiers and 140,000 French soldiers were rescued. Almost all their equipment had to be left behind in France. The Germans were now sitting on the other side of the Channel. Winston Churchill had become British Prime Minister and we listened to his beautiful, stirring orations.

WARTIME LONDON

After July 1940, with the departure of the two little Koerner boys and the beginning of the air raids, I had a very hard time finding a job with children in London.

The bombardment of London had started and most children were evacuated. The barrage balloons had been up over London since the beginning of the war.[17] The German Air Force focused their attention on England. There were daily attacks, but after the Battle of Britain on September 15, 1940, the Germans attacked mostly at night. The air raid alarm sounded every night at dusk and the "all clear" at dawn. There were nightly attacks until November 3, 1940. Nazis attacked every night with at least two hundred planes. Many parts of the great city of London—the docks, the East End of the city, and residential neighborhoods—were severely devastated. But life, somehow, went on, even during air raids.

During the London Blitz, I lived in an old house on Nassington Road in Hampstead. Distant relatives of mine, Pali and Rita, were renting there. After the fall of France, the British started interning "enemy aliens." Most of these were men. Many of our friends were now on the "Isle of Man," an island in the Irish Sea known for its mild climate. Pali, too, was interned on the Isle of Man.

---

[17] Barrage balloons were enormous blimp-like balloons connected by wires to military ground installations. They were used to prevent enemy aircraft from flying too low for precision bombing.

Rita was pregnant and evacuated to the country. She asked me to stay in their rooms.

The house belonged to Olga, the widow of a white Russian general. Russian aristocrats were always visiting her. Anna Pavlova's former lover, a French count, and Madame Kerensky were frequent visitors. They were just some of the interesting people I met at Olga's.

Olga was a sweet friendly woman. She spoke little English and did not realize that it was customary to clean one's rooms even if one no longer had servants. She had been spoiled in Russia (before the revolution) and had not the vaguest idea how to perform household chores without servants. Her rooms were never clean, but the samovar[18] was always going and no sooner did she hear the key turn in the door than she would poke her head out of her room and ask if I wanted "chai" (tea).

Besides Pali and Rita, she rented rooms to several young women with whom I made friends. At night we met in the downstairs dining room. We spent the evenings knitting or playing cards. When a bomb came whistling down, we all met under the dining room table. After we heard the thud of the explosion, we would reemerge with our knitting or cards around the table, never mentioning the bomb that had just gone off somewhere nearby. At night, we slept in what had been a wine cellar a long time ago.

There had been bell pulleys in this old house. Every time a bomb went off in the vicinity, all the bells on the pulleys started to chime. It was eerie.

In August, there was a devastating raid on the City. One could see flames leaping up for miles and the fires lit up the sky. Even in Hampstead several miles away, you could read a newspaper by the fire-lit sky.

---

[18] A samovar is a Russian urn used to make tea.

On September 15, 1940, a beautiful sunny day, the German Air Force made an all out onslaught against London. This was the Battle of Britain. Plane after plane came swooping down over London. I was in someone's garden when it started. We all watched as if we were in a trance. The British Hurricanes and Spitfires came to our defense.[19] We saw a German plane being shot down overhead. It came spiraling earthward. The pilot bailed out and dangled from his parachute, silhouetted against the summer sky.

Hedy who had lived with a relative came to see me one day. She was very upset. Our relative, Aunt Fritzi, had been very fearful during the raids and had gone to a nearby air raid shelter. Hedy and two young girls were alone in her house. They heard a bomb whistling down and dashed into a broom closet under the stairs. The house was a total loss, but the girls survived unscratched. Hedy's heavy trunk was thrown clear and was found later undamaged many yards away. Air raid wardens took the shaken girls, who had barely escaped with their lives, to the shelter where Aunt Fritzi was. Instead of being elated to see the girls alive, Fritzi started crying, bemoaning the loss of her possessions.

After Hedy was bombed out, she came to stay with me. I still did not have a job. All children were evacuated from London and I was only allowed to work in private homes.

During the Blitz, life in London went on rather normally, even the social life. One still went out for tea. One day, Hedy and I visited friends. While having tea, the air raid alarm went off. I wanted to be home. Our hostess tried to prevail upon Hedy and me to stay there and wait for the "all clear," but we left. We could hear the

---

[19] Hurricanes and Spitfires were British fighter planes.

droning of the German bombers overhead and, of course, we saw them. As we entered the house on Nassington Road, they released their bombs. Actually, they were land mines—the latest in destructive weapons.

We were safe in the house, but the street we had just walked on was gone. There was a big crater. All the houses were totally demolished. The convent across the street was a heap of rubble. The habits of the nuns were fluttering from the now leafless trees. A bathtub protruded from a window. All the nuns were killed. The dust was terrible. The front steps of our house were gone, so was the roof. We had no light, no electricity and no windows. But we were safe. The bombers were flying so low they may have seen Hedy and me walking. Were these bombs meant for us?

After that, relatives insisted that Hedy and I take shelter in the Underground. (Since I did not rent there—I was staying at Rita's request—I was only tolerated in Nassington Road. After Hedy was bombed out she did not have a place to stay.) It was awful to sleep in the Underground on the hard dirty floors. The trains ran until midnight and traffic resumed at 6:00 a.m. Every time a train went by it created a terrible draft. Strangers were snoring, wheezing and sneezing around me. I was cold. The few available toilets were absolutely awful and the lines endless. I was much more afraid of catching some dreadful disease in the Underground than of the bombs so I returned to the house on Nassington Road. Half of London lived underground during those days. The deep tunnels of the Underground saved countless lives. The air raids during that period were very severe. Later the Germans threw incendiary bombs on the great city.

All kinds of shelters had been developed. The Anderson shelter was safe against the blast. The Morrison shelter was a reinforced table but strong enough to hold up the ruins of a small house. In spite of the ferocity of the attacks, London withstood. Life went on and the worst was soon over.

During this period I spent a lot of time with mother's cousin, Lucie Rie. She was an extraordinary woman, a great artist and potter, and a wonderful human being. Since 1939 she had, and still has, a studio in one of London's mews (former stables for the gentry's horses). Her living quarters are upstairs; her showroom, workroom and bathroom are downstairs. Very steep stairs connect the downstairs with the upstairs. Besides being a fabulous artist, Lucie has always been an outstanding hostess and cook. Rations or no rations, she entertained a lot.

During the war years, she worked in an optical instrument factory during the day. Before going to work in the morning and at night, she made pottery and blew glass. She made buttons and pins and other high fashion articles from glass. My cousin Herta, Hedy and I stayed with her one weekend and wanted to help her. When Lucie was at work, we cleaned and picked up the glass particles from the studio floor. Where should we put them? There were two large trash cans in the studio and we emptied the dustbins into the cans. Poor Lucie, she kept her precious irreplaceable clay in those cans. She said little when she returned. She did not complain, just set out to lift the glass from the clay, slowly and carefully.

During the Blitz when I visited her, I usually stayed at her place on Albion Mews. I slept on a couch in the showroom. When I woke up I often found people sleeping on the floor or under her Morrison shelter people who had not been there when I went to bed. Lucie had many Bohemian friends and, during an alert, rather than taking the train back to where they lived, they came to stay at Albion Mews. She had a very interesting set of friends. I always enjoyed my visits at Lucie's. There were always guests. I remember once spending a whole night chatting with a young, charming Australian who was later killed during the war.

Lucie treated me as if I were her child when I visited her. We had very strict rations during that time, one egg per week. She always welcomed me with her rationed egg, a very special treat. An incendiary bomb hit her mews during the Blitz. Of course, the damage has long since been fixed, but when I visit her now and run my foot over the floor, I can still feel where the bomb hit, almost fifty years ago.

One day during the Blitz, as I was walking in Kensington, a very large car came to a halt in front of me. I looked in and saw the Queen with a lady. I smiled and curtsied and got a smile and a wave from the Queen.

Soon after my arrival in England came a letter from Jancsi, from a ship lying in Southampton. He had stopped in England on his way to Bolivia and wanted to persuade me to go with him. He was not permitted to land but would send me papers to join him later. Marriage, however, was not mentioned. I did not know what his purpose was. He did send the papers, though. The Bolivian embassy notified me that they were mailed, but the papers never arrived. War had broken out in September 1939 and the boat, papers and all were torpedoed and went down.

Then Jancsi concocted a new scheme to get me to Bolivia. A friend of his was to come to England on the way to Bolivia. He was supposed to marry me and take me with him as his wife. On arrival we were to get a divorce. The letter was intercepted by censors and referred to Scotland Yard. I was called to Scotland Yard and interrogated. I put on my blue hand-tailored suit, which had been made in Vienna, and was very elegant. The question was strange: How come a domestic could afford such elegant clothes? Scotland Yard suspected a white-slave traffic scheme. They dismissed me and advised me to remain in London for further questioning.

In the meantime, in October 1940, the Blitz on London was in full swing. I had lost my job and waited for Scotland Yard to contact me. I never heard from Scotland Yard again, could not find a job during the bombardment of London, and had no money.

Jancsi's friend did show up, but I did not want to have anything to do with him or, for that matter, with Jancsi. The Scotland Yard episode shook me to the core. I did not have money to travel to Bolivia. (I do seem to remember that he was going to send money for the boat fare.) I was too scared to venture on the high seas with U-boats roaming the oceans. I was cross with Jancsi for endangering my life in London or at sea. Of course, he could not have known any of this. I did not want to write to him anymore, I was through with that business. As it turns out, we did not communicate with each other for more than twenty years.

The British during those hard, trying times were wonderful, calm and ready to help. Somehow, life went on and had some normalcy. They sang their war songs—"Laundry on the Siegfield Line," "Roll out the Barrel," "Tipperary," etc.; and you did not have to wait for buses, strangers gave you lifts. No sooner did a bomb drop, and people were ready to help. They were always there with kindness and a cup of tea. As grim as times were, we saw human kindness and generosity. The spirit of the British was so remarkable. To say it with Churchill: "This was their finest hour." London just carried on. People went to work; trains and buses were on time (almost always); hotels, restaurants, department stores were open; and yet, the bombs fell.

One day, I found myself in terribly devastated London with a most glorious view. It was foggy and the destroyed buildings were shrouded in fog. The sun was breaking through the mist and illuminating the dome of St. Paul's. Beauty, absolute beauty surrounded by the horrors of war.

Since the house on Nassington Road was so badly damaged and I was without a full-time job, there was no real reason for me to remain in London. (It appeared that Scotland Yard had forgotten about me.) I decided to leave and join my friend Liesl in North Wales. I arranged for my stay in Abergele, North Wales and left soon thereafter.

It was not easy for an "enemy alien" (as we were now called) to move around. I always needed written permission from the city I was going to. Then I had to show the permission to the police station of the location I was leaving; I had to report on arrival and before departure to the police of the town I visited and report to the police of my domicile when I returned. The police always had to be informed of my movements.

As troublesome as it was to obtain, I did get permission to move to Abergele. I was on my way to yet another part of the British Isles.

ABERGELE, NORTH WALES

After many months of air raids, weeks without full-time work, and with great fear and anxiety, I finally traveled to Abergele where my friend Liesl lived with her infant daughter.

Abergele was a rather ugly little village on the white sandy shore of North Wales. The coastline and the beaches are among the best in the world. The beaches were gorgeous, but the jellyfish in summer were enormous. When you looked into the water, all you could see were jellyfish, big, ugly and slimy. To be stung by one is no pleasure.

Wales is very different from England. Even the people are very different—more intense, not as easy-going as the English. When the population spoke English they spoke in a strange singsong manner. Their accent was hard to understand. Among themselves they spoke in Welsh, a very different language from any tongue I knew on the continent. Words could be a line long and often contained many double "ll's" that sounded like "chl." The Welsh are very neat and clean in contrast to the English. The people of Abergele, probably, had never seen foreigners before and there was something new to gossip about—the refugee population.

If you walked on the street on a weekday morning and called Mrs. Evans, one-third of the women in the street would turn toward you expectantly. If you called Mrs. Jones, another third would turn toward you. If you were to call Mrs. Williams the rest would turn around! Abergele was somewhat of a paradise. War had not come to it.

I stayed in a very small cottage. It was spotlessly clean, although there was no running water in the house. A Mrs. Evans was my landlady. She spent most of her time polishing and cleaning. The house had no bathroom or toilet. One had to use an outhouse. In the cold winter of 1940-1941, it was pretty grim at night. The gas heater and light had to be fed pennies.

Liesl was in a deep depression. Like most Austrian and German male refugees, her husband had been interned on the Isle of Man. The British could not tell the good guys from the bad guys and interned most men and some women; but all were treated well. They were away from bombs and provided with a much better climate on the Isle of Man. Some of the men were later shipped to Canada and Australia and, for many of them, it was the beginning of good productive, prosperous lives in their new homelands.

In Abergele, I was able to get away from the war and be with Liesl who was almost unable to take care of her baby. I helped as much as I could, which really amounted to washing a lot of diapers and laundry. I had no income except a little help from the Czech Refugee Committee. (When members of the Czech government fled into exile, they were able to take some of their funds with them and distributed that money to people who had recently left Czechoslovakia.) But it was barely enough money for anything.

Liesl was affiliated with an organization that trained halluzim for migration to Palestine.[20] These future hall-

---

[20] Young people who worked on the land in Palestine were called halluzim. They were very similar to kibbutzim (people who worked on kibbutzes).

uzim received training at Gwrych Castle, a huge pseudo-Gothic structure above Abergele on a promontory overlooking the Irish sea on one side and the North Sea on the other. The landscape was lovely and the mountains were covered by heather, all pink in spring and summer. Liesl went up to the castle for her meals and brought food down for me. I managed until I found a job and until Aunt Fritzi joined me. Fritzi's husband and son were also on the Isle of Man. For her son, it was a blessing in disguise. He was able to finish high school, start university courses and, later, became a well-known scholar. It was fun to live with Fritzi. She was a marvelous cook and concocted terrific meals from potatoes and carrots. Once a week we shared a small piece of meat.

I soon found a job, again with German refugees. The Klieger family lived in one of those shabby "bathroomless" little cottages. They did have a faucet in the kitchen, however. I helped with all the household chores. There were three children, (including a sweet little newborn baby), a husband and wife and mountains of laundry that had to be boiled. They had an upstairs and a downstairs. The first thing I had to do in the morning was to carry the chamber pot, full to the brim, down the steep stairs to the outhouse. I was so nauseated by this task every morning, I almost threw up.

My wages were small, five shillings per week and lunch. I worked very hard, but in the evening when I came home Fritzi had a delicious meal, prepared from our sparse rations, ready for me. We made friends with a lovely Welsh school teacher, Miss Jones. She had us over for tea, homemade scones and bread with jam every Sunday.

There was a sanatorium for victims of tuberculosis nearby. A sweet Viennese refugee, a young doctor, was a patient there. She had worked in the sanatorium as a doctor until she herself caught the dreadful disease. I visited her a couple of times. I felt so sorry for her and, yet, I was scared. I had had lung problems as a child and decided it was foolish of me to expose myself to this awful disease. She died soon afterward. I felt terrible to have let her down. She was all alone.

I never dated, but came close once. The chef of Gwrych Castle (a German refugee) asked me out. We were to meet in Llandudno but when I arrived he met my bus with another girl, a glamorous blonde whom he had met in the meantime. I was somewhat disappointed but figured that he thought he could expect more from that girl than from me. Llandudno is a beautiful resort with big hotels, and lovely, white-sand beaches. You can even see Snowdonia from there.

One day, I saw an ad in the paper for a matron in a private girls' school. I applied and was hired. The job was in Colwyn Bay along the magnificent coast. The job was not right for me. I had to run the household and there were fifteen boarders, all teenage girls. I had a terrible time getting the girls to go to bed. It was the spring of 1941. All clocks had been moved forward two hours—"double summer time." It did not get dark until after midnight. The young girls would not go to bed, no matter what. I was only 23 years old and not very much of an authoritarian. However, I had lovely picnics with the girls along the beach. One day, we took an excursion to Carnaven Castle where the princes of Wales are invested. (Investing was a beautiful ancient ceremony at the medieval castle in which the title of Prince of Wales is bestowed on the heir of the throne.)

On Sundays, I went to visit Aunt Fritzi, her husband and her son, recently released from internment. I went for long walks with them whenever I could. On one of those visits, I saw Mrs. Klieger whom I had worked for and who now lived across the street from Aunt Fritzi. I visited her and her sweet little baby often.

Once, when I was at my Aunt's, we heard a piercing scream—Mrs. Klieger had found her baby dead. It had suffocated.

It was spring and we were far away from the world's trouble spots, but we were able to keep abreast of developments in the world. On June 22, 1941, Hitler invaded Russia. This changed the war situation totally. Hitler had given up on invading England, at least for the moment, and turned most of his attention to the Eastern Front.

My sister Hedy moved to a little town, Leamington Spa, in the Midlands. I visited her and thought it would be better if we lived at least in the same town, and decided to join her there. Being a school matron was not my thing.

LEAMINGTON SPA

(Summer 1941 - Spring 1945)

In spite of the beautiful landscape of North Wales I had been lonely there. Liesl, Fritzi and their families had left Abergele leaving me with no friends. I was too young and inexperienced to be in charge of unruly teenagers and wanted to be near Hedy. I got police permission to make the move.

Leamington then was a charming Midland town. Had it not been for the many soldiers stationed in the area, the blackout, the rations, the news in the paper and on the radio, we would hardly have known that "there was a war on." It seemed so peaceful and the surroundings were lovely.

I moved to Leamington toward the end of 1941. The main street is called the Parade. There is a huge Victorian town hall with Queen Victoria in stony grandeur seated with a crown, scepter and orb in front of the town hall. A lovely green park Jepson Gardens, the pump rooms (rooms in spas for drinking mineral waters), a department store, some small elegant stores, and several hotels all are situated along the Parade.

In early December 1941, I received a letter. I had not opened it yet when someone turned on the radio. We listened to the announcer telling us that Japan had attacked Pearl Harbor. Now America would enter the war on our side. We were very excited. I still held the letter in my hand. It had come via Switzerland to England. It was from Mutti. It was the last letter Hedy and I ever received from Mutti.

She informed us, in veiled language, that she had been ordered to appear at the Main Prague Railway terminal to be taken to Poland. Of course, she could not say this directly in a letter that went through German and British censorship. But we knew where she was going and that she was going to travel with some of her cousins. None of these cousins survived. In December 1941, we did not understand what a transport to Poland meant. We could have hardly imagined what terrible hardships Mutti was to endure.

After my arrival, I found one more short-lived domestic job. Then I was able to change my work permit and go to work for a photographer, Mr. Hamilton. Mr. and Mrs. Hamilton had a nice upstairs apartment. The studio on the second floor was my domain. I did all the darkroom work, mixed the chemicals, and did the retouching and the dry mounting. I kept the studio spic-and-span. I worked there from the end of 1941 until the end of the war. Mr. Hamilton would tell me all the time about his experiences in the British flying corps during World War I. I considered him an ancient man, particularly since he developed all kinds of illnesses, wore a hearing aid and a cap over his sparse hair to keep his scalp warm.

All this, though, did not prevent him from developing a crush on me. Here I was in the darkroom and he outside in the workshop. Life became quite complicated—he pursued me but I could not leave. The Ministry of Labor would not change my work permit. I suspected that he made a donation where it counted and I was stuck in a very unpleasant situation. It was not unpleasant in the beginning, but over the years he developed quite a fixation on me and I dreaded him. Sometimes he would sneak into the darkroom, but I must say, in his defense, that he never laid his hands on me—all was verbal.

Hedy, her friend Luccie Gordian, Luccie's father, and I lived in a dreadfully dirty boarding house in Russell Terrace. Since our wages were small we could not afford anything better. Eventually I moved into a nice room across the street. My cooking was done on a gas burner in my bed-sitting room. I shared the toilet with everybody who lived on that floor. The bathroom was in the cellar and that I had to share with a bum who inhabited the cellar.

Hedy worked "on the top" of the Parade for another photographer and I for Mr. Hamilton "at the bottom" of the Parade. We looked very much alike and, often, people who had taken the bus down the Parade and saw me there could not understand how Hedy could have gotten there so fast.

I spent a lot of time with Hedy and Luccie Gordian during those years in Leamington. Czech soldiers were stationed there and in manor houses outside Leamington. Subsequently, the Czech army was replaced by Belgian troops in Leamington and the Belgians by Americans.

Hedy met her future husband, Vasek, at a dance in Leamington that I also attended. He was a good looking Czech, a tank officer. When they got engaged I became very concerned because their backgrounds were so different. On the day of their wedding, I still sounded alarmed. She could still get out of it but, of course, she would not. Later, she wished she had followed my advice.

It was a small wedding in Warwick's town hall (Warwick is very close to Leamington.) Vasek's English was so bad that he could hardly repeat the vows after the Mayor. The poor Mayor got so confused that he forgot the text of the ceremony, had to excuse himself, stop the ceremony to get his book and start the ceremony from the beginning. I invited the small wedding party to a restaurant for lunch in Leamington.

Before Hedy and Luccie Gordian were married, we often went to Warwick and Stratford-on-Avon. We saw many of Shakespeare's plays. I read them before we went. We saw terrific performances there, and Richard II became my all-time favorite. Often, we rented a boat and went up the Avon, or had tea in Stratford, or a shandy (ale mixed with ginger ale—an English specialty drink) at a pub, the Dirty Duck, after the play.

Walter, a Czech soldier, quite a bit older than me, sent me a telegram to say that he would be in Leamington and would like to meet me. I was delighted. He was very attractive and I was thrilled by his attention. I had not known he was interested in me. In the morning before his arrival I looked in the mirror at the studio and saw that I had a terrible rash on my face, neck, arms and chest.

On the way home from the studio I stopped at a doctor's office. He would not see me as I was not his patient. Under the British Health Service a doctor was assigned to you. Yet, in the afternoon, he suddenly appeared at my door. He felt badly that he had sent me off like that, especially since he realized that I had the measles. I got someone to send a telegram to Walter asking him not to come because of my measles. Hedy too was informed. She did not live in Leamington then. She came to nurse me and brought her husband with her. The three of us were in one room. I was really quite ill and glad they came.

After the war, I bumped into Walter in Prague by chance. He told me that I could have thought of a better excuse than the measles to cancel our date. He did not believe the truth.

Leamington Spa was in Anthony Eden's parliamentary district, but when Eden was sick Winston Churchill came to Leamington to canvass for him. I did not expect to see Churchill but as I walked back to the studio from lunch, I was enveloped by a large crowd, carried forward and pushed through. A car with a running board was rounding a bend. The crowd pushed me ahead and I had the choice of being on the running board of the car or under it. The running board seemed the better choice.

So there I was on the running board of a big old limousine. Winston Churchill, with his cigar, stood in the car behind me with camera crews in the car behind him. The cars soon came to a stop in an open area. Churchill, standing in his car, began to speak. He was perhaps five feet away from me and I was the next object in his field of vision. He directed his entire speech toward me as if he were speaking only to me. The cameras were busy filming this scene and I was told afterward, again and again, that I was seen with Churchill on a news program. Before every movie, they showed the latest news and there I was with Churchill in the news. I regret to say, I never saw myself with Churchill.

Every night for years, we listened to our radio to follow the war news. At first the news was dismal and terribly discouraging, but with the German reversal at Stalingrad hopes for an Allied Victory increased. We followed the Russian campaign, the North African seesaw desert campaign, the air war against Germany and the slow progress of the Allies from Sicily up the boot of Italy.

During the night of June 5, 1944, we heard hundreds of planes flying overhead. In the morning, they returned, still flying in formation. By the broken formation, we could tell that many failed to return. Even though there were so many planes missing, the sky was still full of them. We knew something had happened, something immense. The invasion of Europe—D-Day—had arrived! We sat glued to the radio and cheered the brave boys. All the long, hard preparations paid off. There were still setbacks to come, but finally this awful war that cost so many lives was winding down.

As the victorious Allied armies advanced into Germany and concentration camps were liberated, the terrible crimes that the Germans had committed against humanity—in the name of racial purity—were revealed. We were not aware that Mutti was one of the victims.

A sweet old Czech couple lived on the same floor that I did. When they moved, Mrs. Curtis, a nurse in the Pumprooms, moved in. She was a charming jovial Scotchwoman. During the London Blitz her house was destroyed and her two children were killed. She and her husband escaped injuries. She had her children's teddy bears on her bed. She often invited me to eat with her. Several times she made great preparations for her husband who was supposed to come home on leave, but, every time, his leave was canceled at the last moment. He was again supposed to come home on leave at Easter in 1945. As usual, his leave was canceled. I met her in the streets of Leamington a day or two after the war in Europe had ended. She was crying. She had just been notified that her beloved husband had been killed in an ambush on the last day of the war. I often think of Mrs. Curtis. She was lovely and courageous. Life was so difficult for this good Scotchwoman.

On April 30, 1945, as the Russians were fighting their way into Berlin, Adolf Hitler and his long-time mistress, Eva Braun, committed suicide in Hitler's bunker. Red Army shells exploded in the vicinity where their corpses were burned. In England, we were aware that Hitler's death meant that the end of the war was near. Seven days after Hitler's demise, the German Reich collapsed and allied forces occupied the land.

Then one day it finally happened—the war in Europe was over. The armistice was signed on May 8, 1945.[21] That dreadful, devastating, bloody war in Europe was finally over. VE Day had arrived. The moment we had all waited for had come.

Hitler's "Thousand Year Empire" had fallen. Germany and most of Europe lay in ruins. The news of Germany's surrender was earth shattering. There would be no more bloodshed, no more aggression.

My emotions on hearing the news were very intense. I was elated. During the bleak war years, the word "future" had no meaning. During those years, there was no future to look to. We only lived for the moment and hoped to survive. Now one could plan again, rebuild one's life, think of a future and new happiness. I was filled with euphoria at the glorious tidings.

My first reaction was to run into the street. My emotions overwhelmed me. I wanted to celebrate, be with people, lose myself in a crowd. It seemed no one else shared my sentiment, except Hedy. She was the only other person I met. She came from the top of the Parade with the same idea. But, while people in Leamington were not celebrating, everyone in London was.

---

[21] May 8, 1945 is most commonly referred to as VE Day, the day fighting stopped in Europe.

RETURN TO LONDON

For a long time I had wanted to return to London. I had no real reason to be in Leamington. Hedy, Luccie Gordian and her father had left for London. I was left all alone in Leamington. Even though I wanted to quit and move to London, Mr. Hamilton would not let me go. And without the approval of my employer, the Ministry of Labor and the police I could not leave. As soon as the war was over, he had to take his former employees back. Then, he wanted to let me go immediately without notice—he wanted his revenge. But now I put my foot down and demanded two weeks wages in lieu of notice. I was entitled to that. After I left, Mr. Hamilton sent very strange love poems to me for several months.

I went to live with Lucie Rie and found a job with the famous photographer Lotte Meitner-Graf. Lotte's sister-in-law was Lisa Meitner, the atomic scientist, who had worked on the Manhattan project.[22] When the atomic bomb was dropped over Hiroshima, Lotte Meitner's studio was overrun by the press.

Lotte Meitner had a very elegant studio with an elite clientele. The front rooms and studio were beautifully appointed, but not the darkrooms where I spent much of my time. She was a very strict taskmaster, but I learned more from her about darkroom techniques than in all the

---

[22] The Manhattan Project was the unofficial designation for the U.S. War Department's secret program organized in 1942 to explore and create the atomic bomb.

years before. I was also her studio assistant and was present when she photographed General Smuts of South Africa, many society personalities and politicians, and Yehudi Menuhin, the famous violinist. Menuhin was very shy and could not relax.

Lotte Meitner was all charm in the presence of her clients. The more famous, the more charm. She asked Menuhin to play the violin. He did and we had a wonderful private concert. She took extraordinarily beautiful photographs of him with light touching his hands and his ears. The rest of the picture was in half light. General Charles de Gaulle had been photographed in her studio and ordered hundreds of prints. He had a mole on the side of his face and it was my task to retouch it out on hundreds of prints. It caused me to have nightmares about de Gaulle's mole.

Not long after I started working for her, Lotte Meitner lost the lease on her studio in Grosvenor Square. She wanted to go into business with me. I was very flattered, but declined. Her personality worried me; besides, I had other plans.

I had to go to the Ministry of Labor because I had problems getting permission to work for Lotte Meitner. I was able to get a temporary permit while I applied for permission for permanent status.

When I was at the Ministry of Labor I heard about a job for German/English speaking people working for the American Occupation Forces in Germany for what seemed to be excellent wages, with training in Paris. I would need good pay to take care of Mutti, if and when I found her; and I was more likely to get in touch with her in Germany. The Americans gave me a test, which I passed. (It must have been a Federal Civil Service test.)

The war in Europe was over. Years and years of bloodshed and agony were over, at least in Europe. The most terrible crimes men have ever committed against men were revealed. The stories were in the newspapers, on the newsreels and on the radio.

I went through very difficult times. I wanted to find out what happened to Mutti. I took time off from work to go through the lists of camp survivors that were exhibited in the various Jewish agencies in London, but I did not find her name anywhere. Each camp had their own lists and I spent days pouring over them. Even if she had survived, I could not have found her name because she had remarried in the Lodz ghetto. Rumors had it that she had survived, but we did not hear from her. The rumors had her coming home, but where was home? She was not on any list. Eventually, we pieced the picture together, but it took many months until we realized that she had perished.

We knew that father was alive. We had corresponded with him via the Red Cross. Mother, too, apparently had been able to be in touch with him because, through him, we had some information about her at the beginning of the war. We waited and hoped, but Auschwitz had been her final destination.

VICTORY

On August 6, 1945—as horrible as it sounds now from the perspective of forty-five years later—we celebrated. Colorful paper and streamers floated through London's sky. People laughed loudly and sang songs. Now it seems incredible that one could celebrate such a dreadful event, but, on that day in 1945, we celebrated. We had just heard on the radio that the Americans had dropped the atom bomb on Hiroshima. Three days later, another bomb was released over Nagasaki.

Those bombs created untold misery, death and destruction, but we celebrated with colorful streamers. It meant the end of this long, protracted struggle, the end of the uncertainties and the misery this war caused. Soldiers did not have to be shipped to Japan. The war was going to be over finally and absolutely. This was the end of it, the absolute end. The allies were victorious. The forces of darkness were defeated. Hitler and his evil empire had gone down in ashes and destruction. The war with Japan was concluded. We were happy in the expectation of a good, brave new world. Evil was vanquished.

August 14 was the day that Japan surrendered. Hedy and I were at Lucie Rie's and we wanted to see how London celebrated. And celebrate they did. As soon as we entered Bayswater Road we were carried forward by the jubilant crowd—up Park Lane to Grosvenor Place to Buckingham Palace. The King and Queen, the two princesses and all the rest of the royal family, were assembled on a terrace waving to the jubilant, singing crowd. It was VJ day, Victory Day—victory over all the enemies of mankind, victory over the evils of war.

Hedy and I had wanted to return to Albion Mews but we could not. We were powerless—we were just carried by the multitude. The throng had a will of its own. Strangers were hugging and kissing each other, singing, dancing, drinking, celebrating, jubilating. It was wonderful to be young and alive.

The crowd carried us to Trafalgar Square and stony Nelson watched over it all. We were on Regent Street and Oxford Street. There was no escaping the crowd, not even to find a toilet.

It was the happiest day of all days. The war was over! Over! Over! The enemy was vanquished. Good won over evil! Hitler was dead! We all fervently hoped that a good, new, world would arise out of the ashes of the old, that all the sacrifices were not in vain, that peace was here forever, that the best of times was about to begin.

On August 23, I left England to go to France and from there, after two weeks training, to Germany. I never returned to England on a permanent basis. My time in England was spent mostly during the war. But I have the fondest memories of "this blessed land" and of the English people. I visit there as often as I can. Hedy left England the same day I did. Her husband had been sent to France and as a liberator to Czechoslovakia and she went to join him. We left the same day under different circumstances and to entirely different lives.

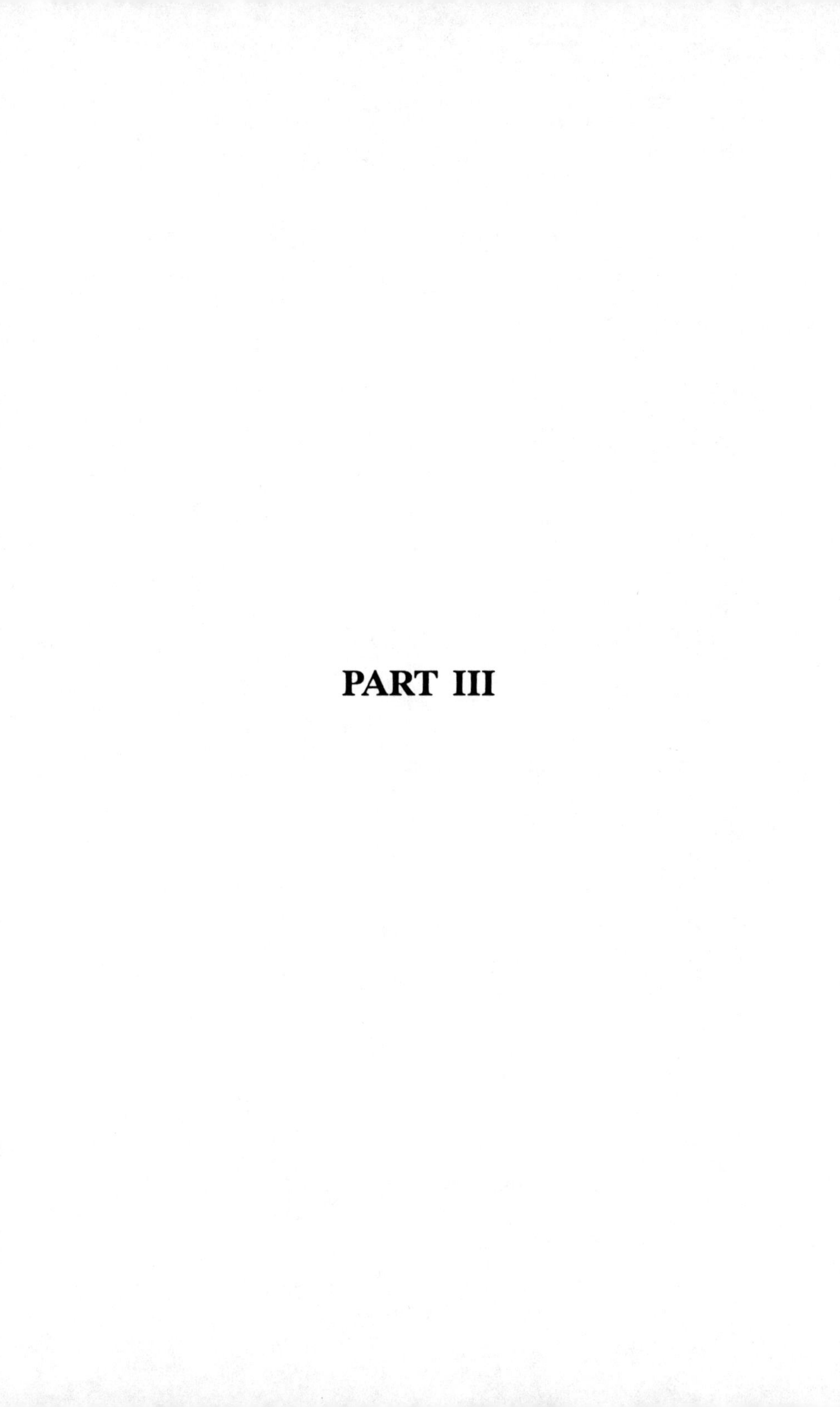

PART III

RETURNING TO THE CONTINENT

In the closing days of the war, I signed up in London to work for the American Occupation Forces in Germany (I had failed to get permission to work for Lotte Meitner-Graf.) I still had hope that Mutti was alive and decided to go to Germany in the hope of finding her there. I needed a physical examination and inoculations. All were administered at the American Embassy in London. While waiting for my turn to get a series of shots, a young woman collapsed at my feet. I recognized her. We had attended the same school in Vienna (Schwarzwald). She, too, was about to start work for the Civil Censorship Division. Gertrud Marle, now Gertrud Blau, has been my friend ever since. Most of the people hired in England to work for the Censorship Division (CCD) were former Austrian or German refugees. The only prerequisite for the job was to speak English and German fluently and the ability to pass the Civil Service test.

It is strange to relate that the best years of my life were spent in war devastated Germany. I left England on August 23, 1945 and found myself with many young people who had been driven out of their native Austria or Germany by the Nazi hordes. We had a lot in common: we were about the same age; our parents had been killed; we had shared the Nazi experience; we were refugees in England; we had no home to go back to; we had somewhat similar educational and cultural backgrounds; and we had not formed attachments during the war. Now we all set out for new ventures. Many friendships were formed that last to this day.

We crossed the English Channel by boat. The boat was not very large but the ocean swells were. I had never been that sick in my life. The waves were enormous. We were lifted up only to be tossed back with tremendous force. We moved upwards and sideways. We tossed and churned. The ocean spray washed over the deck. I went inside. A young girl, Ilse, had joined me. We sat in total misery in a dining room. We saw the sky, the ocean, the sky, the ocean in a sickening repetition through the porthole. People were thrown into our laps and tossed to the ship's opposite side, and again into our laps. Even the naval personnel got sick. I already regretted my decision to leave England. I wondered if this would ever end? It did end in France, in Le Havre.

Army trucks picked us up. American army personnel drove us into Paris where we stayed overnight. The next day we were taken to the quartermaster and issued the uniforms of allied civilian personnel. The uniforms were very smart, not unlike American commissioned officers' uniforms. We were given PX privileges and bought toiletries. We had PX cigarette rations. For a non-smoker like me, they eventually became a source of income. We had the privilege to eat in the officers' mess.

We were driven to Poissy, a very pretty suburb of Paris where we were billeted in an elegant villa, surrounded by beautiful grounds. The vast marble bathrooms had bidets, of course. (No self-respecting French bathroom would be without a bidet!)

The French household employees told us about the German occupation. The same beautiful villa had served as German billets until September 1944.

We started our training immediately. In the evenings we took short train rides into Paris. Saturdays and Sundays were spent in Paris sightseeing.

Can you imagine Paris without traffic, other than maybe an occasional jeep? The French could not get gasoline then. Beautiful, beautiful Paris! We went to the Louvre, Jeu de Paume (at that time it was the Museum of Impressionist Art), and the Champs Elysees. We saw all the wonderful sights of the most beautiful city in the world. All this was ours now.

One evening in Paris, we participated in a big victory parade. We marched from the Carrousel to the Arc de Triomphe. On September 2, 1945, the Japanese signed an instrument of surrender. It was glorious to be part of the great Victory Parade. The war was finally, finally over.

My new life was unconnected to anything that preceded it. Actually, it was to be a good new life. It was the beginning of a normalization of life with interesting new experiences and new friends, and strangely enough, it started in war ravaged Germany.

GERMANY

After weeks of training in Paris, the train carried me toward Germany. For many years I had been an onlooker at world history. What I now saw in Germany was a direct result of what happened, or what was allowed to happen, in Vienna seven years before.

On the way to Germany, we saw a lot of destruction. Everything was strange, so phantomlike. The deeper the train carried us into Germany, the more destruction we saw. The train crossed rivers, slowly, carefully. Most of the bridges were destroyed, just the rails appeared to bridge the river. It was very precarious. We seemed to just balance over the water.

On the way into Germany, we saw rusting tanks and armored cars at the edge of forests. It had been only four months since the end of the fighting. Thin, tattered, starving people were lined along the railroad lines ghostlike, barely moving. I do not know where they came from or where they were going. Their physical condition was appalling. Were they returning German soldiers, civilians, displaced persons (DP's) or released concentration camp inmates? I did not know. They looked like human scarecrows.

Our group of allied civilians in uniform arrived at the railroad station in Frankfurt-am-Main. Suddenly, I saw a group of totally emaciated people—men, women and children—moving toward us. A skeleton of a child ran into our path. Her mother, thin, tall and pale ran after her screaming, hitting the poor child for having run into our way. It was a dreadful dehumanizing scene. I assumed they were people rescued from a camp.

We were taken from the Frankfurt railroad station to Offenbach. There was one railroad bridge and one pontoon bridge over the Main River still standing. All the rest of the bridges were down. Offenbach was only slightly damaged. We were housed in a big compound, always two girls to a room. Ilse was my devoted roommate. And, I mean devoted—she made my breakfast, cleaned my shoes and watched over me like a mother hen. I really did not want any of that attention.

We slept on regular beds with clean sheets, blankets and pillows. The mattresses, however, were made of straw. There was supposed to be an occasional louse in the straw. Maybe that was the reason why I spent so much time in the nearby excellent German beauty parlor and why I suddenly sported henna-red hair.

We received more training in Offenbach and, whenever we could, we tried to go into Frankfurt, the nearest large town. Frankfurt was terribly devastated.

To get from Offenbach to Frankfurt, we again had to cross the river. The pontoon bridge led to Frankfurt's ancient Cathedral and to the Römer. The Cathedral was once known for its medieval beauty. Now it was very badly damaged and had lost one of its two spires. The Römer was once the seat of the Holy Roman Emperors of the German Nation. It was only partially standing. Over the centuries, Frankfurt had been one of the coronation cities of the Holy Roman Emperors. Most of the emperors were Habsburg Emperors, however. Johann Wolfgang von Goethe describes in *Dichtung and Wahrheit* (Poetry and Truth) how he, as a youngster, had watched the coronation of Franz von Lothringen, Maria Theresia's husband, become Holy Roman Emperor. He described the scene inside and outside the lovely Cathedral in poetic detail.

Soon after our arrival in Offenbach, I went to see Goethe's house, or rather what was left of the childhood home of the great German genius, poet and humanist. As I approached, all I saw was a heap of rubble. A woman, an American army nurse, stood on top of this devastation crying bitterly. Two or three walls were standing, a chimney, no roof, but some ceiling beams. A lovely, delicate, crystal chandelier dangled from one of the beams and swayed in the wind. Nothing else was left. The devastation was truly heartrending.

Soon Germans appeared on the scene. They must have heard our voices above the cellars that now served as their homes. They came crawling out from underground where they lived like moles. They told us about the terrible suffering they had gone through under allied bombardment. Goethe's house and Frankfurt are now restored but the results of war are awful and, on both sides, innocent people become its victims.

I had seen awful destruction in London and in Coventry but it was nothing in comparison to what we saw in Germany—rubble everywhere. The Germans were in tattered, worn clothes. They did not have enough food to eat and they wore rags on their feet. They were forever foraging with wheelbarrows in the rubble, in the countryside, in their lovely forests. As a human being, one could not help but feel sorry for the perpetrators of the war.

The black market flourished. Money had no value whatsoever. The only item of value was cigarettes. I remember being driven through a small German town. An army truck ahead of us had come to a stop. GIs were smoking and tossing their cigarettes out of the truck. I observed a rare, well-dressed German hiding in a doorway until the truck pulled away. Then he hurried to pick up the stubs before anyone else could get to them.

The worst destruction I saw anywhere was in the towns of Pforzheim and Heilbronn. The saddest sight was the devastation of the Gothic structures of the once lovely medieval town of Nuremberg. One could only guess how beautiful it must have been.[23] Heidelberg, on the other hand, stood in all its glory. The old castle on the hill overlooking the lovely Neckar valley had been very badly damaged, not in the most recent war, but hundreds of years earlier, in the 17th century. The city occupies a narrow site between the river and the thickly wooded hills. The forests are beautiful, the old university town is picturesque, the castle hills romantic.

Wiesbaden was another city left totally intact. The Romans were the first to make use of the medicinal benefits of the city's famous spas. Many large and rather elegant hotels were built on the ruins of the ancient Roman spas in the preceding centuries. Little resort towns such as Bad Homburg, Bad Nauheim, and Bad Kreuznach were untouched by the horrors of war.

In Offenbach we, the employees of CCD, worked under very pleasant conditions. I had started taking riding lessons and made new friends. Suddenly, orders were issued that some of us, including me, had to move to Esslingen near Stuttgart. We were shipped out by truck the next day. The French had occupied that region and Americans and the Civil Censorship were now moving in.

---

[23] I understand the city has since been rebuilt.

ESSLINGEN

Esslingen is close to Stuttgart in the province of Swabia. The German spoken in that region is almost impossible to understand for a native Viennese. Esslingen was not touched by the war, at least it had no visible war scars. It is a very pretty little town with a spectacular ancient Town Hall. The Town Hall's clock is sensational. It has a complicated mechanism displaying a whole array of figures every hour on the hour. Bells chime and figures move. Children in the street shriek with excitement. It is very thrilling and noisy. A castle is high above the vineyard covered hills with a fortification wall above the vineyards.

We were taken to Esslingen via Stuttgart. Stuttgart, however, had been hit very hard by allied bombardment. Stuttgart is surrounded by rather steep wooded hills. A winding road spirals downward toward the city and traverses the beautiful landscape. The opera, the hotel and the railroad station were not damaged by the war.

We were stationed just outside of Esslingen in what seemed to be blue-collar workers' apartments. There were four women to a flat, which included two bedrooms and a living room. We ate in a huge mess hall and were waited on by German waiters. We worked in what was once a huge machine factory. The compound was situated along the lovely Neckar River. I started work every morning at 8:00 a.m. Between 6:00 and 7:00 a.m. I went horseback riding with a group of young people. Then I changed clothes, had breakfast and went to work.

Work was extremely interesting. I worked for a Viennese American GI, George Blau. He was in charge of the Watch List section. He soon got a promotion and I became the head of the Watch List section.

We had to go through all the mail found in German mail boxes at the end of the war and the mail that continued to pour through the German post offices. We compared the names of the sender and the addressee against a watch list. Among the people we watched were German atomic scientists, who were either sent to the U.S. or kidnapped from streets in Germany and sent to the USSR. Catholic charitable organizations were also high priority on the watch list. They were busy helping former Nazis or smuggling communications to them. Famous Germans were also being watched in addition to the known Nazis.

The CCD, of course, knew about my photographic background and I was soon moved into their photo lab. Before I knew it, I was promoted to chief of the photo section. George Blau became chief of our station in Esslingen and, once he became a civilian employee, he was made the head of all the CCD stations.

In the photo lab we were trained to test for secret inks under ultraviolet light and to find microdots. In order to keep the German censors alert (hundreds of Germans were employed as censors supervised by CCD personnel), we planted microdots in the mail. I became quite an expert at reducing a letter page to the size of a dot on the letter "i" and to blow it up again to its original size. Suspicious letters or watch list discoveries were sent to the photo lab, my domain, photocopied, coded and sent, probably to the OSS (Office of Strategic Service) or G2 (Army Intelligence Branch), both intelligence services. Our original training was by FBI officers.

I read and copied the entire correspondence between a famous German scientist who had been sent to the U.S. and his father. The father wrote beautiful letters and seemed pleased about his son's good fortune to have been taken to the U.S. Then there were the letters of the less fortunate scientists who were kidnapped in the streets of Germany and exported to the Soviet Union. They, too, wrote about their experiences, usually with rather veiled references as to their whereabouts and their conditions. (I was quite an expert at reading between the lines because of the correspondence I had had with my mother between 1939 and the time she was deported in 1941. The letters were sent via neutral countries—the U.S., Bolivia and Switzerland. Those letters had to pass through German and English censors, too.) Some of the scientists from Russia wrote critically, or rather cynically, about their life in the Soviet Union. Others adapted.

I read letters written by one of the great composers of our century justifying why he stayed in Germany and stressing his great friendship with famous Jewish writers. I photographed and read mail by a great German conductor, and by the writer of German children's books who described in one of his letters having been present, somewhere in the background, at the burning of his books.[24] It was all very interesting although we did not make any very profound discoveries or unveil any important secret plots.

Next to the lab was the decoding section and people worked for weeks, sometimes even months, to understand a code only to discover that perverts were communicating with each other. In my section where we developed secret

---

[24] I wish I could share with you the names of these famous people, but that would not be appropriate.

inks, the most unusual we ever found was homosexuals using milk or urine to write love messages to each other.

One time, we found messages smuggled in bars of soap. A breakout of a prisoner of war camp was plotted. That, of course, was nipped in the bud.

Once, in the morning when I came to work, there was an army inspection team in the photo section. To my great horror, we had forgotten to turn off the large drum dryer the night before, and the same prints were coming through again and again. The machine was just about overheating, but nothing further was said about the incident. Thank God!

My next assignment was to take portraits of each employee. I rigged up the micro camera, used low contrast film, stationary lights and had surprisingly good results. I used Lotte Meitner's technique of constant chatter to divert the subject's attention. Presto! I knew every fellow employee and got many compliments on their portraits.

LIFE IN GERMANY AFTER THE WAR

To be in Germany so soon after the war's end was a very strange experience. The juxtaposition of our observations, our feelings, our emotions were incredible. It was an experience unlike any other I ever had.

There was the exquisite landscape, the majestic Rhine River, towering Alps, deep forests, charming little villages with gabled roofs, and the almost total devastation of all the major cities. There was our pleasant life with the American Occupation Forces. There were the Americans themselves.

On the one hand, there was extreme poverty and deprivation. On the other hand, there was an abundance of goods in the PX's. You could not help but feel that the Germans got what had been coming to them; although, on a personal level, you could not help but feel sorry for so many of them. I was constantly torn between hate and pity.

Then there was the mistrust. I wondered how they had been involved? There were always the nagging questions: What had they done during Hitler's time? How much did they know? What did they know? Whom did they harm? Whom did they help? What did they do? Had they been involved in the horrendous crimes? It was a terrible dilemma not to be able to trust people. They all professed not to have had knowledge of anything. Millions *had* to be involved in the outrageous crimes that were perpetrated. Looking the other way was a crime in itself. Did not the world leaders, the Pope, Roosevelt, and

Churchill turn the other shoulder, too? They knew exactly what was going on and did not speak up. How was I to judge people? I solved my problem by being extremely correct and polite; but I tried not to get involved with Germans. The CCD employed many Germans. We supervised them but we did not mix with them. Later on, I got to know some Germans quite well, and liked or disliked them for their individual qualities not just because they were Germans.

In contrast to our very pleasant life in Germany (due to the fact that we worked for and were housed by Americans), the Germans continued to have very hard times. The cities still were heaps of rubble. Slowly the surviving soldiers returned from prisoner-of-war camps. Food was at a bare minimum.

In the cities, stores did not even exist. By the time I left Germany in 1952, reconstruction was in full swing. In the beginning, they were too stunned, lacked the equipment to move the rubble, lacked the initiative, lacked everything.

In the first years after the war, the Germans were moving around a lot. The trains were crowded. Were they searching for relatives, for food, for a place to stay? I observed terrible scenes. I saw young Germans, probably returning soldiers, being lifted out of trains, armless, legless, just heads and trunks of bodies. How could one not feel terribly sorry for such a ruined life, however innocent or guilty the poor creature may have been? To go through life like this? The shame of it all!

I had seen maimed men in England during the war. There was a big military hospital in Leamington Spa and I had observed five young men going for a Sunday afternoon stroll on crutches with just five legs between them. In England I saw airmen often with terrible facial wounds. But that was not as startling as seeing legless and armless men with only a trunk and head. I had never seen such a sight before.

War and its consequences are simply awful. It is no solution to anything. How can it even be contemplated? Will we never, ever learn? Do we need weapons at all?

One of the most moving experiences I had was the first Yom Kippur service in the bombed out synagogue in Frankfurt in 1945. The synagogue's roof was gone. I do not know if it was because of a bombardment or Kristallnacht. American army personnel were downstairs, but upstairs the women's gallery was almost empty. There were a few army nurses, some CCD women, and one or two half-Jewish women or non-Jewish widows of Nazi victims. There were no German Jewish women upstairs and no German Jewish men downstairs. All the Jews had disappeared. The terrible tragedy!

LIFE CONTINUES

Provided we had travel orders, we could travel very comfortably through the American Zone of Occupation or even abroad. We often went to the Bavarian Alps, to Garmisch-Partenkirchen, to Berchtesgaden, to Rissersee, to all the charming Bavarian resorts. We went skiing on the Zugspitze and watched Americans fraternize with German girls, which was strictly "verboten." We often were invited to officers' dances. I became an expert in dancing the polka. Young officers took us to see American football and baseball games. I could not make heads or tails of either. I was able to figure out basketball because I played something similar during my Vienna school days. We gave many parties in our little apartment. Ilse, still my roommate, was a good hostess. We also were invited out a lot.

I belonged to a group of young people who were very fond of music. Some were even professional musicians in their "real life." We went to many wonderful concerts and the Stuttgart Opera. One of the young men in the group had been the first violinist with the Boston Symphony. He had stayed on in Germany to save enough money, with the help of cigarettes, to purchase an Amati violin. I do not know if he ever did.

The Stuttgart Opera, at that time, gave excellent performances. Former members of the Berlin Opera ensemble had taken refuge in Stuttgart and the performances were of a very high caliber. There was a problem, though, in getting to the Opera. The bridges across the Neckar River were down.

We only went to the Saturday and Sunday matinee performances. We hopped a short ride to the river, then walked across it on a pontoon bridge and picked up the train to Esslingen on the other side.

One day, two or three of us in uniform were hitching a ride toward the bridge. We had no other transportation choices. Suddenly, a huge car stopped with four Russian generals in it. All four got out, kissed the ladies' hands and invited us into the car. They let us out at the bridge, got out of the car, kissed our hands again and drove off. I must add, that was at a time before the Cold War.

I had another experience with a Russian officer, much more scary than the first. I went with a group of people by train to the hotel on top of the Zugspitze, Germany's highest mountain. From there, I took a cable car to just within a few feet of the summit. I tried to climb up to the cross on the very summit of that high mountain. Suddenly there was a place where one had to jump to get to the other side of what appeared to be an opening or a cliff. A young Russian officer stood on the other side and stretched out his hand to help me across. I jumped and he caught me, but, as I jumped, I saw that I was propelling myself across a chasm thousands of feet deep. It seemed as if the mountain had split open. I got to the summit and to the cross. Someone had to help me down by another route. I was too scared of what I had seen and had to avoid that terrible abyss. A few days later, one of the girls from work attempted to do what I had done. She missed and was never seen again.

Besides Alpine vacations, I did a lot of traveling. My friend Louise and I had a very lovely vacation in Italy. We were the first tourists after the war on the Island of Capri. The whole island wanted to profit from us and offered their services. We were followed, serenaded, guided and helped.

The CCD had hired many Danes and I went to Denmark as the guest of one of my co-worker's parents. I spent ten days there. Her father was a marine biologist. His beautiful home contained huge tanks of the most gorgeous specimens of fish from the South Pacific. Her mother gave me the grand tour of Copenhagen.

In 1946, I met my father, as pre-arranged, on a train on the way to Geneva. He gave me a little gold watch on that occasion and we stayed in a very elegant hotel along Lake Geneva. With him, only the best was good enough. Soon, we were joined by his brother, my charming Uncle Oscar, the famous violin teacher. He was world famous as a master teacher. Among his close friends were music greats and the Queen Mother of Belgium, Elisabeth. He was on his way to judge a violin competition in Geneva. I visited him soon afterward, in the autumn of 1946, in Amsterdam, where he resided in a lovely small house. He was a fabulous host and, through him, I met many Dutch artists. I fell in love with this wonderful, inspiring man and we stayed in touch until he died.

Father took me to the Palace of Nations in Geneva and it was there that he "explained" himself to me. He answered the accusations I made against him in June 1938 when I last saw him, before I left Vienna. He had much to say about the fact that he did not have the benefit of a dowry when he married my mother (it was lost in war bonds). And, he felt cheated because my grandfather did not let him become a partner in the brewery.

I suppose what I had said still rankled him in 1946. After our time in Geneva, I visited him in Vienna. His sister, Else, was still alive but her daughter and son-in-law perished in Theresienstadt. Father and Aunt Else wined and dined me in Vienna. Suddenly, father was very protective. When I went to the theater at night, he picked me up, unexpectedly, to insure my safety. For so many years he had cared little about me. Now he was being uncharacteristically concerned about my safety.

Vienna was occupied then by the Americans, French, British and Russians. My father took me to the Prater (Vienna's huge amusement park) and there I saw strange, dirty-looking, disheveled creatures. Father explained that these were Russian soldiers. Another time, when I tried to take a taxi, the driver motioned to me to hurry up. Russians were running toward him from a different direction and he tried to avoid them.

It was so strange to be back in Vienna after so many years. I went to our former home in the third district, Weyrgasse 7/8. As I opened the door to the building the tailor who had had his salon on the top floor was going out. He said, "Guten Tag, Frl. Back, wie geht's?" ("Hello, Miss Back. How are you?") just as he had done for years. He said it as if nothing had happened, as if the world had not rearranged itself totally in the past eight years.

The porter took me to our former apartment. It was now two flats. Both occupants were very worried that I would want to have our former home back, but, of course, I had no such intention. I just wanted to take one more look at my childhood home.

Vienna had been damaged by the war but not like London or German cities. The second district was badly destroyed. St. Stephan's Cathedral had been severely damaged, the roof had caved in. Otherwise, Vienna had changed very little. I had forgotten many of the details, but walking the charming streets was like unrolling a carpet of memories. Suddenly it was all there again.

In 1946, I was able to get into the Nuremberg trials. I saw the defendants of the big war crimes trials but could not attend an actual session. I was able to attend a proceeding of the doctors' trial and General Milch's trial. It was hard to follow without knowing what preceded it. You needed to spend much more time there to make sense out of it. The instant translation interested me most.

I also visited Hedy in Prague twice. She lived in a very nice apartment that had been vacated by fleeing Germans. A bust of Hitler was found hidden in the oven and the Nazi woman had left her beautiful fur coat behind in the closet. Hedy now had a lovely fur coat and a sweet little daughter, my niece Jeanny. Our friend, Luccie Gordian, also lived in Prague with her husband Harry, her daughter Eva and her grumpy, but sweet, father.

The government in Czechoslovakia was still almost democratic but there was a strong Russian presence and the Communist party was the strongest party. They soon took over. Our former brewery had passed from the hands of the Nazis to the hands of the Communists without us getting a penny for it. Later, after an endless struggle with the German Restitution Authorities, we received a small compensation for the money two German brewers had actually paid for the brewery in 1939, but the Nazis had confiscated it.

REQUIEM

In Prague I met a woman who had been on a transport from Lodz to Auschwitz with Mutti. She told me how brave Mutti had been in the Lodz ghetto, how she cheered people up with her little stories, anecdotes and jokes, and how she had suffered when her new husband had been taken away from her. Although Mutti was on the same transport to Auschwitz with that woman, Mutti was never seen again once they arrived at their destination. Poor Mutti. It was the last gassing in Auschwitz.

The woman told me her own story. She had twin daughters. They all were supposed to hand in their jewelry before entering the gas chamber. One of the young girls was unable to remove her ring. Her sister and mother tried to help her. As hard as she tried, she could not get the ring off her finger. The portals of death, the doors to the gas chamber closed. The girls and their mother were saved by a tight fitting ring. They did not know at the time what had been in store for them.

Writing about all this makes me so sad. We had a kind, wonderful, brave, intelligent, educated, witty mother with a funny sense of humor. She deserved much, much better from life than she received. Who in the world deserves such a terrible fate such as cruel premature death? She should have enjoyed life, us, her grandchildren, beauty, the music she always loved, kindness, and all the good that life has to offer. She deserved better than the bad marriage to father, years in the ghetto, and her terrible end in Auschwitz. As I write this I am choked up with tears. Mutti, you will not be forgotten.

So it all ended. The members of my once large and otherwise kind family who survived never expressed sorrow. No one ever wrote to say that they were sad about what had happened. Of course, it took a long time until we realized that Mutti would not return. She just faded away, no funeral, no condolences, no visits, no flowers, no memorials, no speeches, no mourning, no hugs, no letters; nothing, but bittersweet memories and belated grief.

I am proud of the fact that I was able to prevail upon father to have her name engraved at my grandfathers' tombstone at the Central Cemetery in Vienna as my wedding gift.

Mutti, farewell! Who can believe in justice? In God in Heaven after such evil deeds? Not I. Not in God in Heaven, only the ancestral brutal ape. To overcome that ape in us is what makes us human.

Mutti, you will always be on my mind. This writing is meant for your grandchildren and great-grandchildren, to keep your memory alive and so our descendants will know about life and death in the first half of the twentieth century.

CCD ENDS

In early 1947, the Civil Censorship Division started to cease operations. The plant in Esslingen was being closed. I was moved from Esslingen to Pullach (a suburb of Munich), and I had to say goodbye to many of my CCD friends. Many of my former colleagues returned to England or Denmark. The American personnel returned to the States.

I suppose I was lucky to have been retained and sent to Pullach. Pullach had been a SS camp for years. The barracks were very comfortable, charming little huts situated in a beautiful forest. The mess hall, too, was surrounded by big fir trees. No one could imagine that evil deeds were hatched in such lovely surroundings.

Munich is a very attractive city. The Isar River meanders through the outskirts. The Alps are only an hour away.

I was again in charge of the photo section. Photocopying then was an entirely different operation than it is now. It was much more photographic with lights and film that needed development in a darkroom. Photo paper, too, had to be developed under red lights. It was a much slower and more complicated process than it is now.

I was still copying letters, classifying them, checking for secret ink, making reports, supervising and often photographing the staff.

All this soon ended. The CCD in Pullach was also being dissolved. Employees were being returned to the places from where they were hired. I was returned to where I started two years ago—to Offenbach. Offenbach was the last of the many Civil Censorship stations. I was in charge of the very last Civil Censorship Photo Unit. I understood that it would not be long before this unit would be closed, too.

What to do? I had planned to go to America. I had applied for a visa when I first emigrated to England. A relative had given me an affidavit. I sent some of my savings to America, but my luggage was sent to England to the home of Liesl's parents.

I intended to wait in England for my American quota to be called and to emigrate to the States as soon as possible. But I was really not quite sure what I wanted to do next. I just knew I could never go back to Vienna for good. The thought of going to America on my own was very scary.

Then my friend Louise suggested that I apply for work with *Stars and Stripes*, the American Army newspaper in the U.S. Zone of Occupation. By then, I had a rather extensive photo lab background and could run any photo lab. I had a very good German camera, a Rolleiflex, and had been quite successful in portrait photography.

I applied for work with *Stars and Stripes* and had an interview with Kenneth Zumwalt, the Managing Editor of the paper. He was extremely nice and showed me around the photo lab which was in total disarray. Film was strewn all over the place, prints were everywhere, and there was no filing system at all. He said he would love to hire me to clean up the place but that he had no opening. If an opening occurred he would let me know. He suggested that I extend my stay in Germany. I interpreted this as a very polite brush-off. I went back to Offenbach and, as I still had accrued leave to be used but no more work, I extended my stay by traveling and returned every few days to check the mail.

Traveling was extremely cheap for army personnel and I did not need much encouragement to travel. I went for the second time to see Hedy in Prague, to Switzerland, and to Brussels. When I returned to Offenbach, there was Ken Zumwalt's telegram: "Please report to work November 1, 1947." That was the beginning of the most wonderful period of my life.

STARS AND STRIPES

My job with *Stars and Stripes* was the best, most interesting, most challenging I have ever had in my life. The opportunities were tremendous, so were the friends I made. I had a feeling of belonging. Almost all my CCD friends had returned home and I had the opportunity to make many new friends, most of them American. Many of them have since become very famous in the newspaper world—editorial writers, TV personalities, etc. The Zumwalts became my lifetime friends. (Ken's new book *Stars and Stripes* has been published and I am mentioned in it.)

In the beginning, I established a negative and print file, set up the photo lab and organized the photos and loose film that were stacked around in odd corners of the lab. I used the skills I had learned at the Graphical Institute in Vienna and those taught by Mr. Hamilton, Lotte Meitner and at the CCD. I did lab work, kept records, supervised the German dark room staff, answered phones and submitted prints to "Editorial."

One day our news editor's wedding gave me an opportunity to prove my photo skills. This one opportunity led to my becoming the first female photographer at *Stars and Stripes*. There was not a single staff photographer in the photo section to record John Livingood's wedding. They were all out on assignment. I took the wedding pictures and, at the party a few hours later, showed the enlarged photographs. After that the assignments came pouring in from Ken Zumwalt's desk with increasing speed.

Ken gave me wonderful assignments. In 1950 alone, I had ten cover pictures in the Sunday Feature Edition of *Stars and Stripes*, more than any of the men who worked there. I continued to run the photo lab and made sure that the prints of all the photographers were submitted to Editorial on time.

The paper was published in a small brewery town, Pfungstadt in Hesse. Pfungstadt was really more a village than a town. It had no distinguishing features except the 16th century town hall and two or three renaissance buildings adjoining the town hall.

During the summer months, a pair of storks took up residence on the steep roof of the town hall. They improved the already existing stork nest, they hatched a baby stork, raised it, taught it to fly, and, when the baby was ready, they all flew south again. The rumor had it that they flew via Gibraltar where there was a yearly great stork assembly to North Africa. However that may be, the pair spent their summers in Pfungstadt. Every year, one of the *Stripe's* photographers was assigned to photograph "stork life" in Pfungstadt. This had to be done from one of the houses with a gabled roof across the street from the town hall. It was not an easy task to climb up on the roof with the telephoto lens and get the most advantageous stork family pose. It usually took the photographer a full day to accomplish this assignment. Thank God I never had to photograph the stork family from that high roof.

Housing for the *Stripes'* staff had been requisitioned. We were eight girls to a house. A maid was assigned to each house. In addition to the maid, I shared a housekeeper with another girl. She made our breakfast and kept our clothes and shoes clean. For her service, we paid Liselotte in cigarettes. She was a very nice, upper-middle class, German woman, the daughter of a manufacturer from East Germany. She had been raped by several Russian soldiers, fled from her home in East Germany to the American Zone and eventually died of her injuries.[25] She was a very sweet woman.

The Press Club was called Chateau Meaux (the brewery owner's rather elegant villa). We took our meals there and the French chef outdid himself every day. Soon *Stars and Stripes* moved its facilities from Pfungstadt to a small airstrip near Darmstadt. Our billets were moved to Darmstadt.

After the paper was put "to bed" about 11:00 p.m., our social life started and went on until the wee hours of the morning. We started work about 11:00 a.m. We were young and had lots and lots of fun at the Chateau Meaux. There were many *Stripes* parties and lots of flirting.

The most important things were the wonderful friendships we formed. We lived pretty much in isolation in this small Hessian town. We somehow functioned as an extended family, sharing all our joys and sorrows. Zumwalt, although quite young then, was the father figure. (At Christmas, he still publishes a yearly paper, the "Zumwalt Zeitung." All the former staff's news is in there but, unfortunately, the obituary column grows from year to year.)

At *Stripes* we worked hard. But our work was appreciated by our colleagues and the people in the American Zone who read our paper and wrote appreciative letters.

Soon after I started work in 1947, a young, blond man with a white cat under his arm entered the photo lab in

---

[25] I don't know the exact nature of all her injuries, but at that time, rape victims often got very bad infections. I think she died from those infections.

Pfungstadt and announced that he was Jerry Waller, the new photographer. He turned out to be very brilliant and educated. He had an excellent sense of humor. He did not know it then, but his goose was cooked. In England, in Old Windsor, a fortune teller, a tea-leaf reader, told me that I would marry a blond man from overseas and that his last name would start with a "W." Well, this was my man. For a long time I resisted being friendly with him. But . . .

Eventually we did get married in the little old town hall with the stork nest. First, we lived in the Bahnhof Hotel in Darmstadt and later in a lovely apartment at the edge of town. We had a view of a large game preserve.

MY PHOTO ASSIGNMENTS

Soon after I started work for *Stars and Stripes*, there was a very bad plane accident in the French Alps. One of our photographers was to go out and photograph the rescue attempts. Al Burchard, an editorial writer, was to go out with him. There were not enough parachutes on the plane. Burchard was bumped. Carrol Sprague, a young photographer, with his Leica camera photographed the scene. The crashed plane was spotted and he took excellent pictures. However, his plane flew too low and crashed at the very spot the first one had gone down. The camera was thrown clear and all the equipment and the film were undamaged. His pictures were published in the paper, but he was no more.

Ken Zumwalt gave me extremely interesting photo assignments. The money conversion in 1948 was one of them.

The Germans had to turn in their Reichsmarks for Deutche marks at a rate of ten to one. They did not like it a bit. They lined up at the banks growling and I had to photograph them. They swore and spit at me. They later learned that the money conversion started their prosperity and the Wirtschaftswunder (an economic miracle).

During my tenure with *Stars and Stripes*, I photographed several fashion shows, including one of Christian Dior's. I photographed one session of the United Nations when they met in Paris at the beautiful Palais Chaillot. General George Marshall was there, as was King Faisal in his flowing elegant desert robes. I got a unique photograph of the Eiffel Tower through one of the windows of the Palais Chaillot.

I photographed Anthony Eden (former British Foreign Secretary who later became Prime Minister) when he arrived at Rhine-Main airport. But my photo could not be used because I did not realize that Jerry was taking a picture of Eden from the other side of the arrival ramp, and he was in it.

A very moving assignment was the celebration of Israel's independence, the foundation of the new State of Israel, in May, 1948. The festivities took place in a DP camp (Displaced Persons) near Stuttgart. There was much happiness, dancing and singing. Most of the recently freed concentration camp inmates, poor homeless souls, had Israel to go to now. I, too, was extremely happy. The dream of freedom in their own homeland from almost two thousand years of exile was now fulfilled. The Jews could go home again and all this happened in our lifetime. The prophecy was fulfilled. The next day seven Arab nations attacked the infant state.

In the summer of 1948, I was assigned to photograph the Salzburg Festival. I had planned to climb into the tower of the Salzburg Cathedral, just before *Jedermann* (a play) was to start, and photograph the audience. As I ascended the tower with my big camera, I heard someone coming down and suddenly there he was—Death! I screamed and Ernst Deutsch, a famous actor, who was getting ready for his first appearance in the window of the Cathedral, laughed out loud at my scare.

One day, the great Russian composer, Dmitri Shostakovich, arrived at Rhine-Main Airport. When he saw the press descend upon him the poor, shy man tried to hide. I had a chance to photograph him, though. I got a rather good picture of him and we even had a little conversation.

Every year the "famous" female-photographer, Lizbeth Back, had to photograph the first baby born in the American Zone. This annual assignment included a baby born in Salzburg a few minutes after midnight on January 1, 1949.

I was on my way to Austria. I was supposed to meet my Father and his friend, Prince von Lippe, after my "baby" photo assignment. The Austrian border official refused to recognize my international travel papers, my American official travel order or my press card. (I was stateless at that time.) I had entered Austria with the same papers before. I became hysterical. After all I had an assignment. I accused him of being a Nazi. His superior was called because I now had slandered an Austrian official. All this was settled peacefully, however; but I cried buckets of tears. By the time my Father and the Prince and the chief of the Salzburg editorial office came to pick me up from the railroad station, my face and eyes were red and puffy. This was very unprofessional conduct, but the terrible Austrian memories had been conjured up in my mind. But I did get my baby picture.

Another assignment took me to a little country hospital where a poor German woman had given birth to quadruplets—four beautifully formed little girls wrapped in cotton. They had no facilities in that little hospital for such a rare birth, no incubators or screens to keep sneezing photographers out of direct contact with the babies. The next day they were all dead.

In 1949 the photo section was very busy processing photos of the Berlin airlift. Almost all the photographers were sent to Berlin except those of us busy processing their output. The Soviets had stopped all rail and road service between Berlin and the West. The Western Powers had initiated a large scale airlift to bring supplies to this enormous city.

In spite of my many assignments I was still in charge of the photo lab. Jerry, in the meantime, had become chief photographer.

One of my favorite assignments occurred in September 1949 when Howard Kennedy, a *Stars and Stripes* reporter, and I were assigned to cover the opening of the Parliament in Bonn. There were some delays in Wiesbaden and we arrived later than anticipated only to find that the *Life* magazine staff had grabbed the admission tickets assigned to us. Howard found a seat in the gallery, but how was I to get my pictures? I noticed an opening in a window of the "Bundestag" (the Lower House of the German Federal Parliament) and climbed in to the amusement of the assembly. Everybody laughed, but I got my pictures of Adenauer (who was chosen chancellor on that day), Ehrhard, Schumacher, and others. Germany was very lucky to have a politically astute man leading them in time of need.

Another assignment involved following Tyrone Power and Linda Christian on their Bavarian honeymoon. They were guests of American generals and I had to pick them up at their messy, untidy room at the elegant Hotel Berchtesgadener Hof in Berchtesgaden. He was terribly handsome and charming. She looked rather uninteresting until I developed the pictures. She was very photogenic.

The army wined and dined them in lovely restaurants. In a restaurant at Chiemsee, I stayed in the background and photographed them. Tyrone Power told a very funny story about a time he was to receive an award somewhere in South America. He made a speech and, during it he felt something fuzzy and soft pressed into his hand. Looking down, he realized it was a shrunken head!

One assignment I enjoyed was photographing the Battenberg (Mountbatten) stallions. I was the only woman to photograph these gorgeous horses. The duke's family wanted to use my pictures for a calendar and I was offered the opportunity to ride any horse of my choice as often as I wanted. Zumwalt, however, did not let me submit the pictures for the calendar. It was against the paper's policy. He did not cater to royalty.

The same thing happened again after I photographed the old Wittelsbach Castle in Berchtesgarden (the castle belonged to the former King of Bavaria). I received a letter from the former King's secretary. The King liked my pictures and wanted to have some copies. Ken, however, did not give his okay.

I photographed the carnival in Strasbourg and Munich. In Munich, I took my pictures wearing an evening dress. Hedy was with me. The hotel where the festivities took place was built on old Roman ruins. I snooped around taking pictures and opened the door to what once had been the cubicle of an old Roman dressing room. I do not know who was more embarrassed, the lovers inside the cubicle or I. Photographing all the celebrations was very interesting. Some of the Germans told of how they had hawked all their worldly goods to be able to participate.

John J. McCloy was the military high commissioner of the American Zone. He requested to be photographed by me whenever he was in public. I was invited to parties at his home. When I photographed his family, I had lunch with the McCloys. Mrs. "High Commissioner" became a cover picture for the Sunday Feature Section. Mrs. McCloy was Mrs. Adenauer's sister.

In the spring of 1950, Trevor Voorhees, the Undersecretary of the Navy, was due to arrive at Rhine-Main airport. None of my male colleagues were in the photo section when the assignment came in so I was sent to photograph his arrival. A general awaited Voorhees, an honor guard was lined up at the airfield for his inspection, and German civilians watched the proceedings. I wore a thin red summer dress and carried the big, heavy "Speed Graphic Camera." I had not the faintest idea what an inspection of the honor guard would be like. The general and the undersecretary popped in and out in unexpected places. I ran toward them, and then the elastic of my panties snapped—quel malheur! I held on to the camera with one hand and to my panties through my dress with the other. I did not want, absolutely did not want, to step out of my panties in front of the general, the undersecretary, the soldiers and the Germans. I was the only female on the field and I am sure they all knew what was wrong. Somehow, miraculously, I got an excellent picture of Trevor Voorhees. (I could not have taken a picture under worse circumstances.) His secretary wrote to Zumwalt for a copy. This time Zumwalt gave his permission. *Time* magazine used my picture shot under such adverse circumstances.

I was always given a German driver for my picture assignments. Once, I was sent to Heidelberg where Cary Grant was making a film with Ann Sheridan. I had photographed her the day before in Frankfurt, but now it was Cary Grant's turn. I do not remember the name of the film they were making. Because certain conditions had to be met, we had to wait and wait. A streetcar had to round a corner, the sun had to burst out of the clouds, and only then could Cary Grant jump on the streetcar. The conditions never combined that afternoon, but it gave me a chance to have a long chat with Cary Grant. He was devastatingly handsome and extremely nice and obliging.

One assignment gave me the opportunity to speak with Cecil Beaton's photo lab assistant. At that time, Cecil Beaton was a very famous English society photographer and stage set designer. The lab assistant told me how poor the quality of Beaton's negatives were and he talked about the dark room tricks he had to use to be able to print from them. The results, however, were spectacular. Beaton was one of the highest paid photographers in the business. His pictures were well composed and elegantly attractive.

In 1950, I also photographed the well-known Hollywood movie queen, Constance Bennett, at her home near Wiesbaden. She was married to an army lieutenant colonel and had a rather plain looking little daughter. They invited me for lunch and her picture became a cover for the Sunday Feature Section.

Another one of my cover pictures was of cows being "taken off" pasture across the Königsee by boat. They later were driven to farms. The light rain that fell enhanced the picture. The shepherdess held an open umbrella. The mountain landscape in the background was partially hidden by rising clouds. The waters of the lake were dark and sinister.

An American film company was filming in a convent near Wiesbaden and I was assigned to photograph them. Anatol Litvak was the director and Oskar Werner was the star of the film. They were working on the film, "Legion of the Damned." The film was a great success, but appeared under another title. I don't remember the name. I was very impressed by Litvak. He worked with a German crew, an American executive staff and a French actress. He constantly switched from English to French to German to Russian. His directions were given with patience, kindness and understanding. My pictures were published in the Sunday Feature Section. One picture became the section cover.

Another time, I was assigned to photograph General Patton's handsome son, a lieutenant colonel. I was at the Rhine-Main airport when he arrived. When he saw me with my big camera, he became very abusive and extremely rude. He threatened that if I used the camera he would grab it and smash it over my head. I knew he meant it. He was not worth my camera nor my head.

In 1950, I photographed castles in the American zone of Germany for a little magazine *Stripes* published, "Castle Tours." At Cat Castle, situated above Mouse Castle along the Rhine, I was bitten by a dog. (The wound became infected and I was sick for ten days with a high fever.) Among all the castles I photographed, Meersburg was my favorite. The Emperor Napoleon had it built for the Empress Josephine. It was an enchanting little castle in the lovely little town of Meersburg along Lake Constance.

In the spring of 1950, I was sent on a Mediterranean cruise to Italy, Rhodes, Egypt, and Greece. American Express sponsored the cruise. They paid for my trip and *Stars and Stripes* published the pictures. In Egypt, I tried to photograph a street barbershop where men wearing fezzes crouched on the ground while being shaved by barbers with long barber knives. Suddenly, they saw me with my camera and came running at me with their open blades. I stepped behind a truck that shielded me from them. Moslems are not supposed to be photographed, but an assignment is an assignment and I did the best I could to get my pictures without offending them too much.

During the same trip, I took pictures in a mosque in Cairo. My camera was slung around my shoulder and I released the shutter without really seeing what I was doing; but, somehow, in that defused light, I got interesting shots. The pyramids became the subject for another cover of the Sunday Feature Section of *Stars and Stripes*.

The trip included seeing Athens one day. Later that evening, I went back and climbed the Acropolis with a newspaper man. It was a unique experience. We were alone. Not a soul was around. We were at the foot of the Parthenon, the sun was setting, the sky was bathed in gold. These are the kinds of moments that make life worth living. This was certainly one of them.

My strangest assignment for *Stars and Stripes* was with the now well-known writer and Pulitzer prize winner, Nan Robertson. We were assigned to cover the story of a German peasant woman by the name of Theresa Neumann. Theresa was supposed to be suffering the stigmata of Christ and to subsist only on the host and wine.[26] At Easter, she was heard talking in Aramaic, an old biblical language no longer spoken. When we saw her she was in a trance-like state. From the very outset, it was a strange, upsetting, and unexplainable experience. At least I could not explain it. It was mystifying.

We drove through the soft, rolling, pretty, early-spring landscape of Bavaria. Fruit trees were in bloom—the lovely soft pinks and whites of the blossoms, the fragrance was bewitching us. We had a map with us, yet we had an unexpectedly hard time finding the little village of Oberkonnersreuth. We found Konnersreuth, Niederkonnersreuth, Überkonnersreuth, but Oberkonnersreuth somehow escaped us. With Jerry as our driver, we combed the delightful landscape for hours. Finally, we did find it. We saw a tremendous crowd in the village, all waiting to file past the "saint." Many expected to be

---

[26] One who experiences the stigmata of Christ is said to bleed from the same wounds that Christ was supposed to have bled from.

healed by her. Many entrepreneurs and vendors had appeared from nowhere. With my press card, I entered easily. I could hear birds twittering as with Francis of Assisi.[27] Incense and excitement were in the air.

It was a strange, moving experience to see this pale, shrouded figure sitting upright in her bed with blood flowing from her hands and head. I was prevented from taking pictures of the "Maid." In fact, I had to leave her room because of the camera, but later entered it again without the camera. There was more blood, much more blood, on the bedclothes. She was extremely pale. Incense penetrated the air. It was quiet in spite of the throng. One could hear the birds. I know both Nan and I were moved by the phenomenon. There was really no reasonable explanation for it. I was perturbed for days afterward.

On the way back to Darmstadt, we drove along the Neckar River. We saw strange, walled towns, and cherry trees in bloom. Several weeks later, we drove back to this region to investigate these towns, but could not find them. This, too, contributed to the strange mysterious feeling of that Easter Sunday. There was one other eerie circumstance. I was not allowed to take photographs of Theresa, but took pictures of the outside of the house, of the crowd. But, when the pictures were developed, one could see her outline against the window.

Jerry was assigned to follow General Eisenhower on our honeymoon in Paris in 1951. The NATO pact had just been signed and Jerry and John Livingood were to cover Eisenhower. I tagged along. There were long chases at high speeds, but finally we caught up with the Eisenhower party at Fontainebleau where he and Montgomery posed for us. Winston Churchill's son, Randolph,

---

[27] I had always imagined he was surrounded by birds.

and Evelyn Waugh's cousin were with us and their presence made this audience possible. I took some pictures while kneeling in front of Eisenhower. He found that so amusing that he laughed out loud.

The crowning experience of my photo career was meeting Henri Cartier-Bresson. In 1951, I spent a wonderful evening in London with my husband, Jerry. We had been invited to a party given for *Life* photographers by the Capa brothers—Robert and Cornell. (Robert, a fabulous photographer, was later killed on assignment in Indochina.) One of the guests was a photographic giant—the great French photographer, Henri Cartier-Bresson. He and I spent the whole evening talking photography. He was a lovely, modest man, and the most wonderful photographer. He used a Leica camera exclusively and never used flashlight. Every picture he took was framed perfectly and when enlarged it never needed cropping. I was absolutely in awe of his art. It was an unforgettable evening!

RECONSTRUCTION BEGINS

When I came to Germany in September 1945, the major German cities lay in ruins. Hundreds of thousands of Germans, nay, millions were dead; millions were maimed and crippled; millions were homeless; German minorities had been driven out of Poland, Czechoslovakia, Romania, and Russia. Many of them were now in the American Zone of Occupation. People were constantly moving, and searching for relatives, for food and fuel. Germany was in a terrible, terrifying condition.

But General George Marshall's brilliant plan and President Truman's foresight made recovery possible. Eventually, the great German, Konrad Adenauer, appeared on the scene and became chancellor. With the help of the United States, reconstruction was possible and I was a witness to it.

The singular, most important factor that led to Germany's recovery was the currency conversion. For years, money had no value whatsoever. Only cigarettes had value. But it was decided to reevaluate the mark to ten percent of what it had been. Suddenly, money had value again. The stores once again began to fill up with goods. Fruit that had been permitted to rot on the trees was picked again. Food, shoes, cameras and handbags that until now were only sold on the black market for cigarettes started appearing in legitimate stores. My observation was that the money conversion was the beginning of Germany's economic recovery, the "Wirtschaftswunder." Heavy equipment moved the rubble and the rebuilding of the country began.

But a very disturbing event now developed—the Cold War. As I remember, it all started in Berlin. Squabbles arose between the American and Russian occupiers. I am convinced that at the time they were both at fault. With wisdom, patience, goodwill and determination much could have been avoided, but nobody displayed these qualities. It was pure one-upmanship.

When I first came to England, I was shocked to hear comments such as, "We are fighting the wrong enemy." You could hear similar comments again after a long and bitter war had been fought. They said, "We fought the wrong enemy."

The situation became worse and worse until the Iron Curtain descended. I am not a politician, but I had harbored some hopes that the Soviets would ease their stance and democratize, and that the Allies would become more egalitarian. It seemed so reasonable. The world could live like brothers in peace and harmony. Reasonableness is not what world politics is made of, however.

It was very discouraging, but now, some forty years later, the situation has eased and I hope it will continue to do so. Maybe "perestroika" will be the answer.

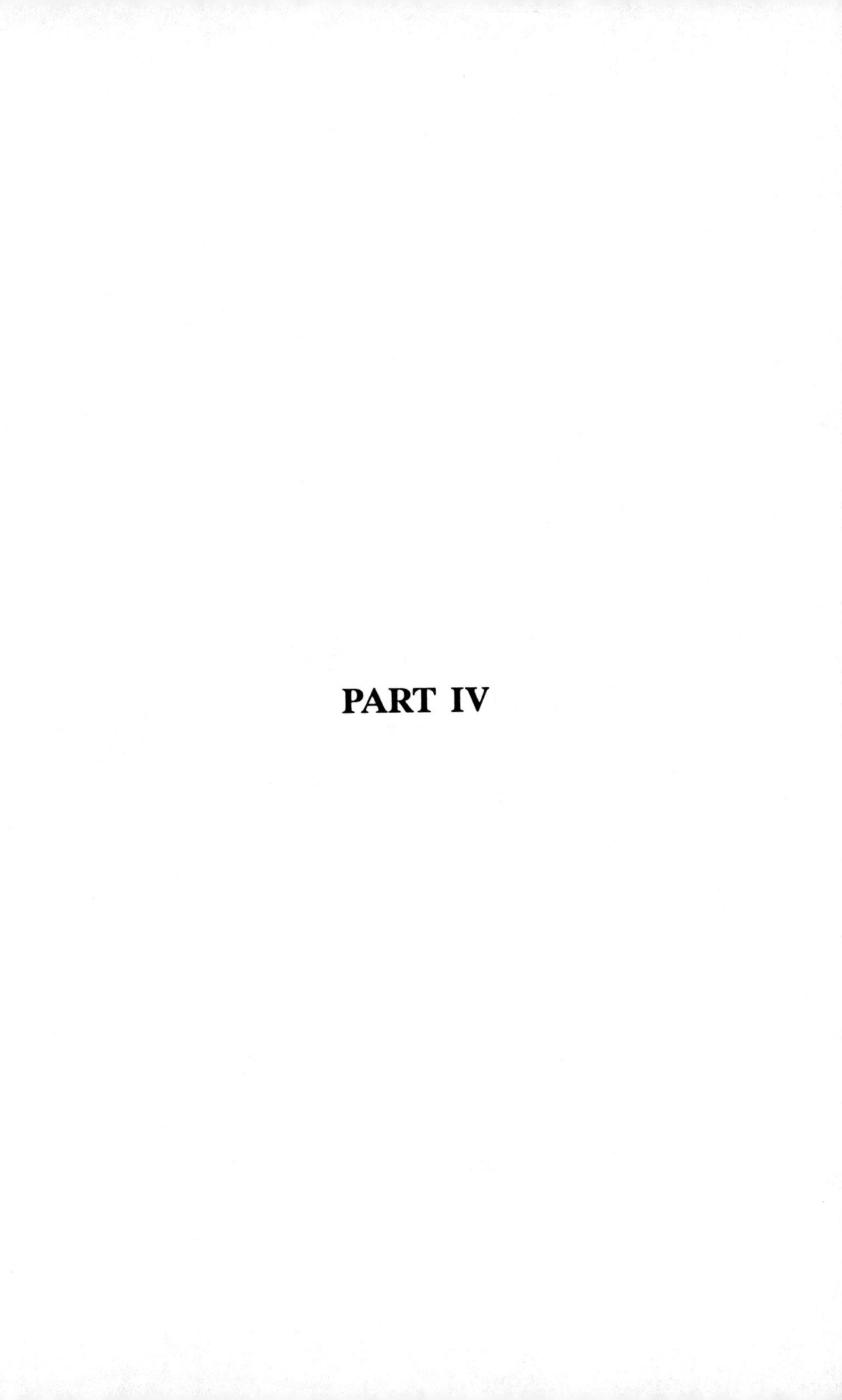

PART IV

WHAT HAPPENED

On the day I went to Germany to work for the "Civil Censorship Division," my sister Hedy and other Czech war brides were repatriated to Prague. Hedy had a very sad first flying experience and will not fly anymore. (Unless I go to see her in Australia once more, I will never see her again.) Hedy and her best friend were among those who returned to Czechoslovakia. The two young women had intended to fly together but somehow were separated. My sister arrived safely but her friend went down with the plane. No one survived.

Hedy and her family settled in Czechoslovakia in 1945, but after the Communist takeover they fled that country. They gave up their comfortable home in Prague, packed and left. They had to seek their fortune in foreign lands and begin anew.

Hedy still had her English "Certificate of Residency," but her husband, Vasek, could not legally leave his native country. He was subject to military service. Hedy and her little daughter, Jeanny, stopped off in Frankfurt on their way to England. They stayed with me in Pfungstadt for several months. Those were anxiety-filled months. Hedy was not sure if her husband could or would actually join her. In the end he did. He had to cross borders on foot illegally, hide during the day and walk at night. He was caught at the Czech-Austrian border. He bribed the border guard by handing over his suitcase. He left his homeland for the second time illegally, empty-handed and for good. He now had no worldly possessions except a box filled with aquamarines. He smuggled them out for Uncle Kurt who had paid a large amount for these gems before the war. They turned out to be nothing but colored glass. Vasek came out of his homeland totally, completely empty-handed; but he came out alive.

He stayed with my Father for some time in Vienna, crossed the border between Austria and Germany illegally and then joined Hedy and me in Pfungstadt. Hedy, Vasek and their little daughter soon moved to Bavaria to a charming little village close to the Austrian border, Bayrisch Gmain. They lived in a shabby room with paper-thin walls and no running water, but had the most spectacular Alpine vista from their window. Vasek had a hard time learning English and German. Hedy had to be the breadwinner. Vasek took care of Jeanny. Hedy worked as a clerk for a sanatorium for tubercular DP's that was run by a Jewish organization, HIAS. HIAS was going to pay their fare to Australia.

After moving from Austria as a refugee to Czechoslovakia, then to England, repatriation, back to Czechoslovakia, and another flight from Czechoslovakia, Hedy now wanted to emigrate to one of the most distant places on earth, to a quiet haven far removed from the turmoil of Europe—Australia.

At *Stars and Stripes* I worked eleven days and then had three days off. With the various holidays I frequently had long weekends and was, therefore, able to travel to Bavaria frequently to see my little family.

My sister and her family were ready to move on to Australia in June 1950. Father, who was now divorced from Lily, came to say goodbye to Hedy with his new bride, Christa (only two years older than me and extremely beautiful). Accompanied by his little daughter he had with Lily, they came to say farewell to the departing family. It was our last gathering of what was left of the immediate family.

Hedy and I said our adieus. She was terribly nonchalant about her impending departure. I had the feeling she was indifferent to our farewells. She just said "Goodbye." I was in tears after parting.

I took the train back to Darmstadt where I lived at that time. *Stars and Stripes* had recently moved to new quarters there. I cried all the way from Bayrisch Gmain to Munich where I had to change trains. Then, again, tears burst forth on my journey to Darmstadt. I was heartbroken. When would we meet again?

It was nineteen years later when we met in Australia. Too much time had passed. Any closeness between us was gone by then. We just could not make the connection anymore. Our lives had developed too differently and there were still some unresolved jealousies from our youth. It just did not work. We often speak on the telephone, however. Vasek died a few years ago of cancer. Jeanny lives in Sidney. She is divorced and has a very brilliant son, David. Hedy gave birth to another daughter in Australia, Anne. Today, she is a well-known international photographer (of all things!). Unfortunately, the beginning in Australia was very hard for them, but now they love living in gorgeous Sydney and they are very happy.

Father died in 1957 leaving Christa with a very young son, Peter, who is not much older than my son Tom. Christa had to raise Peter without a father. Peter is a theater director in Vienna now and very successful. Christa died recently.

Lily lives in Vienna with my half-sister who is a doctor and is married to an immensely rich manufacturer. Her husband spurns the Jewish connection and will not have anything to do with his Jewish sisters-in-law. They move in the still anti-Semitic circles of Vienna's high society.

Liesl moved from London to New York with her family. She received a Ph.D. and taught at New York University for many years. She visited me in Los Angeles last year.

My cousin, Herta, is a doctor in South Wales and, as a hobby, she raises and breeds Lippizaner horses. Her children, except her scientist son, live in England. Her brother, Ernst, works at the Academy of Science in Vienna. He is married to a charming Viennese painter. He loves the beauty of Vienna, but hates living there. He is planning to return to England when he retires.

Ernst wrote me recently with his observations.

"Shortly before leaving Vienna we went to Brno and to Uherske Hradiste and Jarosov. In Brno I did some lecturing at the Technical University; while Uh. Hradiste was an extremely sad sentimental journey. Our house is totally dilapidated and seeing it meant losing all the beloved people associated with it again. First and foremost, of course, my father and mother, but your mother was not far behind. Fritz's house is gone altogether and his beautiful garden is a dump now."

All my Back cousins have passed away. Once in a while, a Belgian descendant of the Backs will visit Los Angeles. All the old uncles and aunts are dead. The old generation is gone. Several of mother's Wolf cousins are still alive though. Lucie Rie lives in London and, at ninety, still makes the most exquisite pots in the world. I talked to her on her last birthday. She told me she received so many birthday cards but did not know who wrote. People mostly signed their first names on the greeting cards.

Our warm family life ended abruptly when Hitler marched into Vienna in March, 1938 and the following year into Czechoslovakia. We all had to flee for our lives. The family fled to the four corners of the globe. Mother's aunts and uncles, whom I dearly loved, were quite old by then. They settled in strange lands with different climates, had to learn new languages and customs. I never saw them again. Those who escaped the Nazis and their evil intentions were the lucky ones. Grandfather's family died in Theresienstadt, so did members of my father's family. Other relatives were murdered in Budapest.

Mother's large family had prospered and flourished for centuries in the territories of the former Austro-Hungarian Monarchy. After the Nazi takeover the family ceased to exist as a cohesive group. To this day I mourn the breakup of our family life. Those who did not perish fled to America, Australia, Argentina, and Palestine (Israel). Some emigrated to England. My beloved great aunts and uncles were lost to me forever. Even though several survived for years, I never saw them again. Distance and war separated me from cousins, uncles and aunts. To me the loss of this warm, loyal, witty family, the family gatherings, the happy family life we enjoyed was a traumatic blow I have never been able to overcome. The memories are still vivid in my mind and I miss those times. Our family life had come to a bitter end. All I have left are my memories of events like my great-grandmother's Hermine Wolf's eightieth birthday party attended by more than eighty descendants and relatives. Because of the losses during the war and the geographical spread of the remaining family, today that kind of event would be impossible.

At the end of the war, there was no relative from this once enormously large, old Austrian family, left in Vienna. Some returned later, but have since died. My half-brother and sister were born after the war and live in Vienna.

The former family home is a museum now owned by the city of Eisenstadt. It houses a collection of Roman and Celtic antiques, old implements, birds, etc. Part of Uncle Sandor's collection forms the foundation of the Austrian Jewish Museum in Eisenstadt, as well as the Josef Haydn Museum.

The vineyards and fields do not exist anymore. Eisenstadt grew and spread over them. One may still see a tree or a lane we knew as children—the world of yesterday infringing on the world of today. All the homes of my family in Vienna are occupied by strangers.

Now my closest relatives live thousands of miles away. Some live in England, others in Israel, in South America, and my sister in Australia. My daughter and her family live in Seattle. Jancsi's and my correspondence was revived many years after the war through a mutual friend in Los Angeles. By then we were both married. We each had a boy, Tommy, and our daughters had similar names. Jancsi had married a woman by the name of Hedy. We exchanged family photographs. He seemed to have prospered, but then he died suddenly under mysterious circumstances. He was in his late forties. He had kept all my letters and his wife found them after his death. His son came to see us many years later in Los Angeles and, through him, I learned about some of the events.

Who knows how this love affair would have ended under normal circumstances. I know how charmed I was by Jancsi, but too many unusual conditions arose in the seven years we were in contact with each other in our youth. It was not meant to be. I last saw him in 1936. I remember the lovely young man and still regret what might have been and could not be.

None of the young people I met in Budapest, Jancsi's friends or cousins, survived the Nazis. mother's cousin, Rosa, her husband, their daughter and grandchild were mowed down by the Nazis in the streets of Budapest, their bodies floated down the Danube. Rosa's son survived and lives in Israel and I hear from him about Jancsi's family.

It was winter and the storks were not in residence when Jerry and I got married in the little town hall in Pfungstadt. The snow was fluttering from the sky. It was extremely cold and the roads were full of ice on our wedding day in 1950.

Within a few months we moved to a charming apartment in Darmstadt. Our son, Tom, was born in 1951. He was an adorable little fellow and a great joy to us. I had a woman to help me with him. Diapers and sterilizing bottles were still a lot of work. Washing machines did not exist in Germany then. Diapers had to be boiled. Grocery shopping meant going from one little store to another.

I was not prepared in any way to be a mother. Oh, I loved little children and particularly my own little ones. I had always hoped to have children. But even though I earned my living taking care of children in England, I was not really prepared to be a mother. As a refugee in England or a news photographer in Germany I did not have an opportunity to see children of friends or relatives grow up. I had no mother to advise me.

When I was pregnant, I spent much of my time knitting for the baby I expected. When I took my little son home from the hospital he wore a beautiful knit outfit—coat, hat, mittens, booties—all matching and in beautiful pale blue. When we arrived in Darmstadt, a thirty-minute drive from the hospital, the poor little fellow had a terrible heat rash.

I was terribly overprotective with my little ones. Somehow I lived in constant fear that something terrible would happen to them, that they would be hurt, or get sick, or simply melt away.

We had a good life in Darmstadt until Jerry became very ill with pernicious anemia, a very serious blood disease. I did not understand what that meant. One day I had lunch with my friend, Nan Robertson. She asked me what was wrong with Jerry and when I told her she burst into tears. I had not understood the word "pernicious" and did not realize we were dealing with a fatal disease. I thought it was just some form of anemia.

We were extremely lucky, though. At the time Jerry got ill, scientists in Darmstadt found a treatment for the dreaded disease. At first, he needed daily shots and later pills. Jerry was too ill to work and we decided to go "home" before the birth of our little daughter. On the ship Jerry needed a daily dose of shots. The disease has now been in remission for thirty-nine years.

A WEDDING GIFT

My father, whom I loved so as a small child, who had taken us on outings to the Prater when we were little, and to shooting galleries to show off his marksmanship, turned out not to have been a good father after all. He was too selfish for that and I developed strong love-hate feelings toward him. I was consumed with jealousy and sorrow when he left us for another woman, our former cook, Lily. He had caused my mother such grief. My parents' divorce was awful. The bitterness between my parents had spoiled my childhood.

I started seeing my father again when I was living in Germany. He survived the Nazis because he had false papers; and had been protected by his marriage to a non-Jewish wife. From 1944 to 1945 he hid in Hungary and reemerged in Vienna after the war was over.

Jerry and I got married in Germany, but father did not attend the wedding although he traveled frequently, nor did he send us a wedding gift. After our son was born, he came to visit us in Darmstadt. No gift. Eventually, he purchased a little squeaky toy animal for his first little grandson.

After a few days, he took me to the side and asked me, since he had not yet given us a wedding gift, what he could get us. I felt awkward about such a belated offer but said that the nicest gift he could give me would be to have my mother's name engraved on my grandparents' tombstone in Vienna and to have the graves attended to. He promised he would do it. The visit went very well. He was all charm and full of little anecdotes. He was a big hit with the ladies at *Stars and Stripes*. After a few days he returned to Vienna. I took him to the railroad station, waved goodbye and never saw him again.

Many years passed by. Jerry took me and our little son to Los Angeles in 1952. Soon we had a little daughter and I was unable to travel for many years. I corresponded with my father and his third wife. He married soon after his second divorce and he died in Vienna in 1957. In 1964, I went to Vienna for a visit and stayed with my half-sister.

Aunt Louise was still alive then. She had returned to Vienna to work at the university there. I wanted to go to my grandparents' grave. My aunt accompanied me. I bought flowers at the entrance of the Jewish part of the cemetery. Business was so slow, perhaps even at a standstill, (probably because there were no Jews anymore) that a big, ugly fight ensued between two flower vendors. They fought over who was going to sell me the flowers.

The cemetery was in terrible condition. In the last weeks of the war there had been heavy fighting around this area. The tombs were badly damaged, the headstones had toppled over. The walks were not repaved. Everything was in disrepair. Wild flowers, trees and bushes were overgrown. There was a wild and tragic beauty. There were hardly any Jews left in Vienna and the cemetery was not in use. My aunt, however, was able to locate the family tombs. Miraculously, they were well tended. And there it was—I had forgotten about the wish I had expressed to my father in 1952. He had had mother's name engraved below her parents' name and under the name of her brother, who had been killed in Russia in 1915: "Margarethe Back, née Braun, born in 1889, died in 1944 in Auschwitz." She was not forgotten.

Here was the whole sad family story. I sat down and cried. My mother's name was there. He had fulfilled my wish. Here was my wedding gift.

GOING HOME TO A STRANGE LAND

Because Jerry wanted to go home to his place of birth, Los Angeles, California, my life in Europe soon came to an end. The years in Germany had been wonderful interesting years. These had been the best times of my life—new friendships and learning experiences, a sense of belonging, lots of fun, but also missed opportunities.

Now, I moved on to another totally, unexpectedly different world—America.

As usual, I was not prepared for this change, and such a drastic change. Of course I had read books by American authors: Steinbeck, Upton Sinclair, Sinclair Lewis, Theodore Dreiser, Mark Twain. I saw innumerable American movies, had met Americans in Europe, even married an American, but I had no mental picture of what lay ahead and was totally unprepared for what I found in America. Americans were and are much friendlier, much easier going than Europeans. In a way, more naive.

In America, "I'll be seeing you" is equally as meaningless as "How do you do?" is in England. "Come and drop in" is just a pleasant way to get rid of you. "How are you?" means, God forbid, don't tell me how you really are. In any case, you have to be well or okay. But when I first came to the United States I did not know the refinements of greetings or goodbyes.

When I came to America on the French ocean liner, the "Ile-de-France" as the wife of an American, I was convinced that I was leaving beauty behind in Europe. Then we entered New York harbor on a lovely sunny day in late July 1952. It was the most spectacular sight I have ever seen. The Statue of Liberty, the skyscrapers, the sun on the water, the excitement, the hustle and bustle were exquisite. I was not prepared for that, nor for the dirty, seedy streets of New York.

Nor was I prepared for California—the wide streets, the small little houses, the distant hills that you could hardly see. Nor was I prepared for the overcast (not to say smoggy) skies. We had been staying with Jerry's parents for several weeks, when one day I was in their garden and looked up and saw that there were mountains I had not noticed before. I got all excited and called for my husband.

"Jerry, Jerry, where did the mountains come from?" Of course, they had been there all the time, but atmospheric conditions had rendered them invisible.

This enormous city had no decent transportation. I did not realize that Hollywood was part of Los Angeles. I had no idea, in fact, where Hollywood was. I had never thought about it.

The brown hills and the climate were a complete surprise. We arrived in summer. I had heard people talk about the wonderful climate. What was so lovely about it though? The summer was pleasant and warm, not unlike a summer in Central Europe. When I wore my warm winter coat in January, people started questioning me.

"Why the warm coat?"

"Well, after all, it is January," I said. Only then did I realize that it was somewhat warm for my coat. But I did "freeze" here, too. I was not used to the terrific difference in temperature between day and night and felt extremely cold in sunny California.

I was also unprepared for all the electric appliances: washing machines, dryers, dishwashers and the like. I did not trust them and went on boiling my son's diapers and hanging them up outside. My mother-in-law thought I was odd, to say the least, and I heard a lot about it, spoken to my face or behind my back, but within my earshot.

I came here during the McCarthy hearings and was convinced that again I was in the wrong place at the wrong time. Like in Austria under Hitler, Czechoslovakia and the crisis I witnessed there, and the air raids in England, I was amazed when it all blew over.

I hated Los Angeles at first. I had lived in large cities before but never in one that was so spread out. I did not drive yet. I had two small children; we had no money; we lived in a rather paltry neighborhood on Venice Boulevard.

Once I learned to drive and we moved into a residential area, away from the busy boulevard, things started to change. I had gained freedom to move, found new friends and started to feel at home.

My husband, of course, had spoken about Los Angeles, about California, about America, about his family. But I had been unable to imagine any of it.

SETTLING IN AMERICA

(1952 - Present)

Jerry's parents had not been told of his illness. For a long time his mother had urged us to come to Los Angeles. One day, while still in Darmstadt, we received a letter from his father. He invited us to stay in their home for as long as necessary. He wrote: "Our home is your home." No sooner did we arrive at their home in Los Angeles than I was told by Jerry's mother that she had not invited us; it was only his dad who did. How was I to know? Jerry was terribly ill and too sick to work. I had a nine-month old baby and was five months pregnant with Leslie. I had not understood the finer points of that invitation.

My previous life had not prepared me for motherhood, nor for a very critical, mother-in-law whom I could never, but never, please, no matter how hard I tried.

Leslie was born in November 1952. Shortly thereafter, we found our little apartment on Venice Boulevard. Jerry was still ill. He was without work for about ten months. Eventually, he found work as a photographer for the Los Angeles County Flood Control District. The job paid little. Most of our savings had been used up by then. I tried children's portrait photography for a while but had to compete with cheap "house to house" photographers, and I started to babysit instead in order to bring in some money.

I loved motherhood tremendously and I loved my two children, Tom and Leslie. They were adorable, loveable little children. I believe they had a very nice childhood in our small apartment and later in our small house. They had lots of playmates on our suburban street. I took them to the beach and playgrounds and enrolled them in all kinds of activities even though we did not have a lot of money.

In 1956, I achieved three milestones—I became an American citizen, I received my driver's license and we purchased our first little house. I was settled now. I had a family and a home. I had arrived. Vienna and my past had receded into the back of my memory.

I spent nice vacations with my children in places like Lake Arrowhead and Yosemite National Park. Jerry, unfortunately, usually was not able to accompany us. He has been sick almost all our married life. (After he recovered from pernicious anemia he developed other problems.) When Leslie was 13 years old, she had a very severe case of pneumonia. She and I went to Lake Arrowhead for a prolonged recuperation period. We became very close then. (It was just like the time Mutti and I spent in Arosa when I was ill as a child.)

Eventually my sweet little children turned into teenagers. In the 60s, that was no laughing matter. Tommy fancied himself to be a flower child. Revolution was brewing in our home and it was directed against us, his parents. It was awful. We went through very rough times, as I am sure many other families did at that time. When Tom was given a low number in the draft lottery, we had an additional worry. Thankfully, he was not called to serve in Vietnam.

Leslie spent much of her teens sequestered in her room, on the telephone and making up and ironing her long blond tresses. She studied as little as she could get away with, but did get a college degree.

I took Leslie to Europe twice—once as a present for her high school graduation and another time after she graduated from college. During those trips she was able to meet Uncle Kurt, Tante Gretl, Lucie Rie, Herta and Ernst. I took her to Eisenstadt and to Weyrgasse in Vienna. Tom visited Hedy and his cousins Jeanny and Anne in Sydney in 1980. I have been back to Europe several times to see relatives, sightsee and for new adventures.

My mother-in-law was very nice to the children but between us there was little understanding. She had expected a submissive, pliable young girl and I had hoped for the loving, kind, refined, educated Mutti I once had. We were both wrong in our expectations. I was quite independent. Our backgrounds were entirely different. She was anything but a loving, cultured Mutti. Whenever I brought up the subject of my lost family with Jerry's mother, there was a block. She simply did not understand; she could not comprehend.

The most liberating event for me was when I learned to drive. It enabled me to work part-time when Leslie entered first grade. The additional income improved our financial situation. I continued with part-time work until the children entered high school. Then I started to work fulltime.

I started to work for the California State Employment Development Department in 1959 and retired in 1981. I worked on a number of anti-poverty programs always with great enthusiasm in the hope I could make the world a better place. We tried with little success to make the unemployables employable. I did enjoy the challenge of the job immensely. I earned good money and thus helped to improve the living standard of my family.

Even though I worked and had two children to take care of, I tried to stay as involved in cultural activities as I could. I was at the opening of the Los Angeles Music Center in December 1964. Jascha Heifetz played Beethoven's Violin Concerto and Zubin Mehta conducted. I sat in the last row, but I was there. As a member of the Los Angeles County Museum Association I attended the opening of the Los Angeles County Museum of Art in 1965.

I met many nice, educated women at work and now have an endless supply of good friends. We go to lectures and classes, to the ballet, concerts, movies, plays and luncheons, do volunteer work and sometimes just chat. I do volunteer work in my old field of employment—counseling.

After I retired, I volunteered to work for the 1984 Los Angeles Olympic Organizing Committee. At first, I was assigned to the audio-visual section. There I established a slide library. (The work was very similar to the work I did for *Stars and Stripes* thirty-seven years earlier.) I found the slides in a similar disarray as the strewn-around negatives at *Stars and Stripes*. I enjoyed working with the young people, the publicity people, the editorial writers, and the photographers. It was deja vu. (The *Stripes* photographers had been much better, though.)

After a while, the Olympic Committee offered me a position as Public Information Supervisor. I worked there until after the Games. We had to give sports information over the telephone. We answered calls from all over the world and in my late sixties, I had to learn a lot about a multitude of sports, their history, their heroes.

My in-laws died in 1974 and 1975, respectively. Our children lost excellent and loving grandparents.

My son Tom is a bachelor. Leslie married handsome, nice John Raftery. They live in Seattle with their adorable children—sweet, serious deep-voiced, eleven-year-old Christopher, and enchanting, saucy, teasing, eight-year-old Lauren. This volume has been written for them. I visit Leslie, John and my lovely grandchildren frequently. I am proud of the fact that my daughter is my very best friend. We have a wonderful relationship.

Jerry, too, is retired. He is not in very good health, but he is busy with his vast stamp collection, his crossword puzzles, and he is still reading two or three books a day and retaining everything he reads. He is a real homebody in contrast to me who always has to be on the go and active.

I often regretted giving up photography in America in favor of Civil Service. Photography and photo assignments at that time were quite incompatible with motherhood. At the time, when I needed to go back to work, I did not know "all the ropes" in my new country yet.

The first years of my life were extremely difficult. My parents' divorce, the Nazis, the loss of my mother, the loss of our family life. Emigration during my early years was so trying, but the American years have been mostly good years. I like the friendly easy-going Americans, and who would not like the California sunshine?

I have lived in Los Angeles since 1952, longer than I lived in Europe. At first, I found the adjustment to my new environment very hard. I not only had to adjust to a new country, but also to being a housewife, a mother, a daughter-in-law, and having to make new friends. I no longer had the glamorous life of working for a news organization, and being in Germany where news happened. But it wasn't too long before *Stars and Stripes* friends moved here and we had a circle of friends once more.

Having been a refugee so long ago has the advantage now that I know people in so many distant places. I visit them and they visit me. When we first arrived in California in 1952, Jerry had a large family. They all have since passed away, but his brother David and his wife Lola are more than relatives. They are friends.

Between 1938 and 1952 I had moved constantly from country to country, from city to city, address to address, even to a new continent. I had gone home to a country I did not know, to a strange city, to Los Angeles, my husband's city of birth, which I hated in the beginning and now love. This is my home now. I still look forward to every new day. I keep very busy, have many friends, attend classes, and read; I even wrote this book. I love cultural things and enjoy seeing Los Angeles grow from a wasteland into a cultured, sophisticated metropolis.

Still, I long for Europe—the charming little towns, the beautiful big cities, the fragrant Alpine meadows, the splendid landscape, the winding rivers and fast little brooks, the majestic Alps, the great art treasures, Vienna, home, Mutti, and perhaps, my youth.